THE SANGAMON

by

EDGAR LEE MASTERS

Illustrated by LYND WARD

FARRAR & RINEHART
INCORPORATED
New York *Toronto*

PRINTED IN THE UNITED STATES OF AMERICA
BY J. J. LITTLE AND IVES COMPANY, NEW YORK

THE SANGAMON

Books by Edgar Lee Masters

A BOOK OF VERSES
MAXIMILIAN
THE NEW STAR CHAMBER AND OTHER ESSAYS
BLOOD OF THE PROPHETS
SPOON RIVER ANTHOLOGY
SONGS AND SATIRES
THE GREAT VALLEY
TOWARD THE GULF
STARVED ROCK
MITCH MILLER
DOMESDAY BOOK
THE OPEN SEA
CHILDREN OF THE MARKET PLACE
SKEETERS KIRBY
THE NUPTIAL FLIGHT
MIRAGE
THE NEW SPOON RIVER
SELECTED POEMS
LEE, A DRAMATIC POEM
KIT O'BRIEN
JACK KELSO
THE FATE OF THE JURY
GETTYSBURG, MANILA, ACOMA
LICHEE NUTS
LINCOLN—THE MAN
GODBEY
THE SERPENT IN THE WILDERNESS
THE TALE OF CHICAGO
DRAMATIC DUOLOGUES
INVISIBLE LANDSCAPES
POEMS OR PEOPLE
MORE PEOPLE
ACROSS SPOON RIVER: AN AUTOBIOGRAPHY
THE GOLDEN FLEECE OF CALIFORNIA
THE NEW WORLD
THE TIDE OF TIME
THE SANGAMON

Rivers of America books already published are:

KENNEBEC *by Robert P. Tristram Coffin*
UPPER MISSISSIPPI *by Walter Havighurst*
SUWANNEE RIVER *by Cecile Hulse Matschat*
POWDER RIVER *by Struthers Burt*
THE JAMES *by Blair Niles*
THE HUDSON *by Carl Carmer*
THE SACRAMENTO *by Julian Dana*
THE WABASH *by William E. Wilson*
THE ARKANSAS *by Clyde Brion Davis*
THE DELAWARE *by Harry Emerson Wildes*
THE ILLINOIS *by James Gray*
THE KAW *by Floyd Benjamin Streeter*
THE BRANDYWINE *by Henry Seidel Canby*
THE CHARLES *by Arthur Bernon Tourtellot*
THE KENTUCKY *by T. D. Clark*

THE RIVERS OF AMERICA

Edited by

STEPHEN VINCENT BENÉT and CARL CARMER

As Planned and Started by CONSTANCE LINDSAY SKINNER

Art Editor RUTH E. ANDERSON

THE SANGAMON

CHICAGO
SPOON
MISSISSIPPI
ILLINOIS
SANGAMON
OAKFORD
PETERSBURG
SPRINGFIELD

CHAPTER ONE

PETRARCH had the Sorgue, but the Sangamon was wished on me. Little Menard County, nearly two hundred miles south and west of Chicago, is after all the Sangamon. Its largest town is Petersburg of about 2,300 population, while Decatur of more than 57,000 people, lying on a bend of the Sangamon forty or more miles east, never had any distinction that I know of for being on the banks of the river. When the town consisted of a few log cabins, a store, a tavern and a courthouse, Lincoln drove through, but didn't stop. He went on west of town and took up residence on the banks of the Sangamon. This has no bearing on the river, or anything else that I know of. But as biographers of Lincoln have dug up everything about his life it might be considered unfair if it were not mentioned. Also if no notice should be taken of the fact that on May 9, 1860, the state Republican convention met at Decatur, in what has become known as the Wigwam Convention, where the declaration was set forth that "Abraham Lincoln is the choice of the Republican part of Illinois." What of it? Time answered the question "what of it?" but then people could ask it. And that was asked in Menard County, where Lincoln was not popular. There he was known as a bank man, a tariff man, a cultivator of the aristocracy, and his Whig party, becoming with caution the Republican party, was not to the liking of the Kentuckians and Tennesseans of Menard. Menard for everything that makes for flavor and happy remembrance is the Sangamon River.

It was here that Douglas came in his strong days when he was building railroads and establishing the University of Chicago, giving it ninety acres of Chicago land and raising money for it. He was a friend of education, not by word of mouth only. He was a whirlwind of energy, as well as a wonderful mind. He often made speeches at Petersburg. There it was that Captain A. D. Wright lived, a captain in the Mexican War who had such adoration for Douglas that he named every one of his children after him, such as John Douglas Wright, Charles Douglas Wright, Adah Douglas Wright, and others. Meanwhile there was Richard J. Oglesby arriving as a "poor farm boy" over at Decatur. He became governor of Illinois, and in the days of the Haymarket riot in Chicago he had it in his power to show clemency to the misguided men who got the rope for throwing a bomb, which they never threw nor procured to be thrown. One time when I was a youth living in Lewistown, near the Spoon River, he made a speech from a platform in the courthouse yard. I was present and heard him denounce as a traitor and a rebel everyone who didn't vote for the tariff, and thereby give the factory men the money with which to pay good wages, which in those days, anyway, they didn't pay, after getting tariff help. The local Democratic paper denounced him as an "ignorant blackguard," and it was true that he was loud and didn't play many strings, except those that sang the praises of the soldiers and captains and statesmen who had put down the "Rebellion." That was the all-sufficient argument at the time by which to elect a Benjamin Harrison to the presidency. They called Oglesby "Uncle Dick." Later his daughter married an Italian nobleman, which, according to some cynics, was proof of the direction in which the bank and the tariff led; while Harrison grabbed Hawaii, and laid the first steppingstone to the Orient.

Let us return to Menard County, to fine hospitality and prairie peace, to the hills about Petersburg, to New Salem two miles away, to the fiddlers and the lovers of horses, to this little political division that sent 1,084 men to the Civil War and many to the Mexican War, many in fact to all the wars. Some of these veterans used to be about the Petersburg square when I was a boy. There was Cornelius Rourke, who lost a leg in the Mexican War and went crippling about from Brahm's Store to Small and Ruddy's restaurant, then to his home in the next block.

I like to think of the names of the Menard County people, such as Snodgrass, Estill, Deerwester, Twaddle, Tuckelson, Gum, Hornback, Godbey, Smoot, Petrie and others. You who never saw this country and this river may yet get some of the scents and sounds of these prairies when the precincts of Menard County are mentioned: Indian Point, Sugar Grove, Rock Creek, Tallula, Sandridge. Wafts from the very soil come up with those names, as well as from accounts of the fish fries, camp meetings, and the stories of Clary's Grove and New Salem. It is not a fond looking back to youth days that keeps me enchanted, not at all—it is magic in that soil, in the plains, the borders of forest, the oak trees on the hills. I am sure that if you should drive through Menard County strange dreams would come to you, and moreover those dreams would tally with mine. If so, does not something float out of that soil, are

FOR A HUNDRED YEARS AMATEUR ARCHEOLOGISTS HAVE DUG IN MOUNDS ALONG THE SPOON AND SANGAMON RIVERS

not the past people of this region "double-lived," having this place on earth and some place beyond, like the poets dead and gone of Keats?

You might think of Cadmus if you were a reflective person and familiar with mythology, for everywhere in Menard County are the graves of soldiers. They were the farm boys who walked off happy to the wars, who were sown in that corruption, and who were raised into the fame of John Brown and the like—incorruptible resurrection! The blood of soldier boys crops monopoly and imperialism, and they in turn crop more soldiers. The lesson can't be learned in this world which always muddles and stumbles.

Both the Spoon River and the Sangamon belong to the Illinois River valley. They are small streams, while the Illinois is navigable and proved to be of commercial importance. John Reynolds, governor of Illinois at the time of the Black Hawk War of 1832, mentioned in his autobiography that "the Indians long before a white man saw the Sangamon country, were apprised of its fertility and rich products. In the Pottawattamie language Sangamon means where there is plenty to eat." That was truly said, for along this river is some of the richest land in the world.

Charlevoix passed down the Illinois River in 1721, and saw the Sangamon River, which empties into the Illinois near Browning in Schuyler County. Charlevoix called the Sangamon the Sa-qui-mont.

The Indian word was probably "Sau-kie-min," from "auki," earth, and "min," good. Another derivation is said to be from "Saukie," the name of an Indian tribe, and "ong" meaning a place; in other words, a river of the Sauks. Another derivation is "sa-gie," meaning a lake, and "mong," meaning a loon.

The Sangamon takes its source in Ford County in eastern-central Illinois, it flows south through Champaign County, through Piatt County, west and south through Macon County, of which Decatur is the county seat, near which Thomas Lincoln took up his residence when he moved from Indiana; then north and west through Sangamon County in which the capital of the state, Springfield, is located; then north through Menard County, where it is joined by Salt Creek in Sandridge Precinct; then west between Menard and Mason counties, and between Cass and Mason counties, then into Schuyler County where it empties into the Illinois River. In all, the river is something more than two hundred miles long. It broadens as it approaches the Illinois River, but its average width is 150 feet or so. In places it is deep, and it is full of treacherous holes, into which unwary people step and lose their lives.

This river winds and bends around heights and hills covered with oak trees and through prairies where the buffalo grass grew in the long ago, but where now and for many years there are distances of corn and oats and clover. It is a beautiful country, and in these days of paved roads and better houses and buildings it is still more beautiful, with a beauty that is not New England's, but a wonderful beauty of its own, keyed by the prairies, groves of oak trees, landscapes of level fields rimmed by forestry.

It is an old land. In the days when Sir Christopher Wren was building St. Paul's, when King Philip's War was raging in New England, Jacques Marquette was searching for the Mississippi River with Joliet. About the time that Philadelphia was founded by Penn, La Salle was exploring the Illinois River country and looking up at the cliff of yellow sandstone from the waters of the Illinois, later called Starved Rock. La Salle established a colony on the Illinois in 1682. His men cut away the forest that crowned the rock, built stone houses, and encompassed the summit with a palisade. This place is no great distance from the confluence of the Sangamon and Illinois.

La Salle found the great town of the Illinois near Starved Rock, and the country about was filled with Indians. They were the Natchez, the Siouans, the Illini, Algonquins, Shawnees, Sauks, Kaskaskians, Peorias, Cahokians, Miamas, Kickapoos, Pottawatomies and others. According to those learned in such matters there never was such a thing as a first race called the Mound Builders. The Indians were the mound builders, and they inhabited the Illinois and Sangamon river lands for thousands of years.

For a hundred years amateur archaeologists have dug in mounds along the Spoon and Sangamon rivers, bringing forth artifacts like flint heads, beads, and the like. Reverend R. D. Miller, a beloved minister of the Cumberland Presbyterian Church at Petersburg, was one of these explorers. Another was Dr. W. S. Strode, who lived many years at Bernadotte on the Spoon River. At Cahokia, near East St. Louis, there are mounds of great extent in which were found pottery of highly developed form and design. Near the center of the area, which contains eighty-five smaller mounds, is an earthwork said to be the largest in the world. It is a truncated pyramid with a broad terrace, and covers sixteen acres. It is 100 feet high, with an east and west width of 710 feet and a north and south length of 1,080 feet. In the mounds near Joliet, called the Fisher group, skeletons with long skulls were found; also short skulls, unaccompanied by artifacts. In the middle levels were found skulls of short-headed people, with many pottery vessels and artifacts of stone, bone and shell. In one of the smaller mounds were short-headed skulls amid iron, brass and silver utensils. Truly this is an old land of many generations changing along the centuries down to historic times.

One of the richest archaeological finds in Illinois, if not the richest of all, was made on the Dickson farm near the junction of the Spoon and Illinois rivers. This was ten years ago or so. The Dickson farm is on a high bluff overlooking the valley of these two rivers.

THEY HUNTED IN THE SANGAMON BOTTOMS FOR DEER AND ON NEW SALEM HILL THEY CHASED THE WOLF

Here, while grading was being done, Indian skeletons were unearthed, and some years later the mound was explored. Two hundred and thirty skeletons were exhumed, but they were left in their original postures, together with their tools, pottery, weapons and ornaments. The excavations revealed five different burial tiers, each of which is supposed to have corresponded to the existing surface of the hill. Later burials were placed over earlier ones until the top of the mound reached a height of fifty feet. Archaeologists from different universities were attracted by the find, and much has been written about it. A museum was built over the mound to house the artifacts and the 20 skeletons that were found in it. Many spoon-shaped shells are found in the Illinois mounds. The Spoon River abounds in these shells, and the tradition is that the river got its name because of the presence of these shells.

Thousands of years before Illinois became a possession of the French crown, before the English flag was run up on old Fort Chartres near the junction of the Illinois River with the Mississippi, before Clark captured Cahokia, before Virginia ceded Illinois to the federal government, these Indians, called Black-sand men by archaeologists, hunted and fished in the Illinois, the Sangamon, and the Spoon rivers. They stood on the high ridges and watched the rising and the setting sun. They roamed the prairies around the Dickson place; they hunted in the Sangamon bottoms for deer; and on the New Salem Hill, near Petersburg, they chased the wolf. They perished in the cold and by disease, and were buried in tier after tier with their shells and their arrowheads and flints. They knew nothing of the white man who was dreaming of China, of the ships that would bring him across the Atlantic. That happened at last. And Illinois was explored by the French, and there was whisky, barter and cheating, and the shedding of blood.

Illinois emerged as a state in 1818, stretching from the latitude of Maine to that of North Carolina, and was peopled from Kentucky and Virginia, until New England began to take a hand in its building. That was due in part to the conflict about Negro slavery. By 1870 the nonnative population of Illinois consisted of 133,290 New Yorkers; 162,623 people from Ohio; 98,352 people from Pennsylvania. The entire South was represented by 206,734 persons. Nearly the whole of northern Illinois was New England. That gave the new Republican party the popular vote in 1858, and later it held political control for many years, particularly after the War Between the States. Yet the Spoon and Sangamon countries remained more or less intact for a long time. They adhered to Virginia, and to Thomas Jefferson, with the result that Menard County developed one of the distinctive cultures of America. Considering that these folk were shaped by the prairie and by the blood of Virginia, it may be said that no breed of people in the whole land was ever more individual, more distinguished by strength and courage, by good will and hospitality, by industry and the independent spirit. It is strange now to read that James Monroe, who made a journey to Illinois in 1785, reported that the Illinois River country and its districts would "never contain a sufficient number of inhabitants to entitle them to membership in the Confederacy." By 1830 Fulton County of the Spoon River had a population of over 1,800 people, Sangamon of the Sangamon River had a population of over 12,000 people, and Menard, which was not organized until the late thirties, had a population of over 4,000. The rich land, the prairies had drawn people from Kentucky, Tennessee and Virginia.

The prairies are vast stretches of meadow, and at first they were overgrown with wild grass starred with lilies, yellow daisies, purple mint. Harriet Martineau, who visited Chicago in the 1830's, was entranced with the silence of the measureless miles of grass and with the fields of wild lilies which met her eyes as she roamed by the shores of Lake Michigan. The prairies may be seen to great advantage around Bloomington, around Springfield, only a few miles from the Sangamon River, in Menard County, particularly around Tallula, and north of Petersburg, where they are hemmed in at the north by the Mason County Hills, a drift of graceful elevations along the winding Sangamon. Once these regions abounded in buffalo, wolves, deer, wild swans and turkeys, cranes and pelicans. Now for long years there has been nothing here but the silence of the grass, and an unresponsive sky in which during the summer months the turkey buzzard wheels looking for carrion. Around the prairie everywhere is the rim of forests, as if they concealed some bourn, some destination. The wolf has been driven from the woods, the buffalo long ago vanished. Nothing remains but the prairie, which like the sea defies change and the works of man. The eye roams the waste and sees barns and houses miles away, some houses that have stood for a century or nearly that. These barns and houses, and sometimes a windmill, seem to speak a silent language of past generations, of the young who laughed and made marriages and grew old, and of the old who looked over this same scene and wondered, as we do, what the earth and the sky mean. For all my love of the prairies I can understand how it was that they affected Charles Dickens so disagreeably, and how it was that some of the pioneer women grew melancholy under the influence of their unchanging mood. It may be that the faded eyes, the drooped eyelids of some of the old women of Sandridge were caused by years of gazing over the level stretches of grass to the rims of forest that seemed to bound a happier land.

Charles Dickens was in Illinois in 1842. He saw the Mississippi River near Belleville, which is below

St. Louis, and at Lebanon near Belleville he stayed at a tavern concerning which he wrote, "in point of cleanliness and comfort it would have suffered by no comparison with any English ale house, of a homely kind in England." At this time McKendree College at Lebanon was a going concern, named for William McKendree, a Methodist bishop and associate of Peter Cartwright. Dickens could not escape looking at the prairies, however much they disappointed him. "Looking towards the setting sun, there lay, stretched out before my view, a vast expanse of level ground; unbroken save by one thin line of trees, which scarcely amounted to a scratch upon the great blank, until it met the glowing sky, wherein it seemed to dip, mingling with its rich colours, and mellowing in its distant blue. There it lay, a tranquil sea or lake without water, if such a simile be admissible, with the day going down upon it: a few birds wheeling here and there, and solitude and silence reigning paramount around. But the grass was not yet high; there were bare black patches on the ground; and the few wild flowers that the eye could see were poor and scanty. Great as the picture was, its very flatness and extent, which left nothing to the imagination, tamed it down and cramped its interest. I felt little of that sense of freedom and exhilaration which a Scottish heath inspires, or even our English downs awaken. It was lonely and wild, but oppressive in its barren monotony. I felt that in traversing the prairies I

IN THE POTTAWATTAMIE LANGUAGE SANGAMON

MEANS WHERE THERE IS PLENTY TO EAT

could never abandon myself to the scene, forgetful of all else; as I should do instinctively were the heather under my feet, or an iron bound coast beyond; but should often glance towards the distant and frequently receding line of the horizon, and wish it gained and past. It is a scene not to be forgotten, but it is scarcely one, I think, at all events as I saw it, to remember with much pleasure, or to covet the looking on again in after life."

Stories of the wonder of the treeless grasslands spread east over the world. Stephen A. Douglas heard of the Illinois country and went west about 1833. Later he said that his mental horizon was widened by the prairies, that his eyes were relieved of the cramp of hills and mountains which they had long encountered in Vermont. At Princeton, in Bureau County, for many years lived John Bryant, a brother of William Cullen Bryant. Princeton is not far from the Illinois River, nor far from Starved Rock. John Bryant cultivated apple orchards. In 1832 William Cullen Bryant paid a visit to his brother in Illinois, and while there wrote the poem entitled "The Prairies":

> These are the gardens of the desert, these
> The unshorn fields, boundless and beautiful,
> For which the speech of England has no name—
> The Prairies. I behold them for the first,
> And my heart swells, while the dilated sight
> Takes in the encircling vastness. Lo, they stretch

In airy undulations, far away,
As if the ocean, in his gentlest swell,
Stood still, with all his rounded billows fixed,
And motionless forever—Motionless?—
No, they are all unchained again. The clouds
Sweep over with their shadows, and beneath
The surface rolls and fluctuates to the eye;
Dark hollows seem to glide along and chase
The sunny ridges.

He noted the mighty mounds that overlook the rivers, and felt that the feet of his horse might be trampling the dead of other days who lived when the Greek was hewing the Pentelicus, and rearing the "glittering Parthenon." By this time the Indians had been driven away to a large extent, and within a year or two of the date of this poem nearly all of them were sent beyond the western borders of the state; and here no more roamed "the majestic brute in herds that shake the earth with thundering steps"; though "this great solitude is quick with life," the "graceful deer bounds to the wood at my approach." He heard "the low of herds" blent "with the rustling of the heavy grain."

CHAPTER TWO

SQUIRE DAVIS MASTERS, my grandfather, came from Overton County, Tennessee, to a farm near Murrayville, Illinois, in 1829. Later, in 1847, he moved to the Sangamon River country, to land about five miles north of Petersburg in the very center of a prairie landscape. The spot is about five miles from the Sangamon to the north, and about the same distance to this river from the east. For from Petersburg the river flows north. It turns west as it reaches the Mason County line, thus making almost a rectangle which encloses the undulating expanse of grass and fields. To the north it forms a rhythm of levels and gentle slopes; to the east the land climbs to some extent; to the west it stretches unendingly to the setting sun. His neighbors, whose houses and barns dotted the landscape, whose land was enclosed by the picturesque rail fence, were the Kirbys, Combs, Watkins, Armstrongs, Hatfields, all people of hearty good will and neighborly kindness. He had several hundred acres of land. To the west of his house was a pasture of sixty acres, where I used to go to fly kites and to gaze at the Mason County Hills five miles north, or at the rims of forestry all around the horizon, or at the thunderheads under which the turkey buzzard gracefully sailed.

Memory is a kind of reading glass under which spots of earth long beloved take on the aspect of something magical, as of a miniature world examined with godlike eyes. So this pasture of sixty acres and the surrounding landscape appear to me as I reassemble the Sangamon River country. The rims of forestry, the distant houses, the Mason County Hills, the rail fences and hedges, the thunderheads, the undulating land toward the house and barn of George Kirby two miles north, all seem like a fairy world as I have recollected the days when I was fourteen to about twenty, and spent every summer working for my grandfather on his farm in Sandridge Precinct in the heart of the prairie.

MY GRANDFATHER HAD SOME OF THE IDEALISM WHICH WE ASSOCIATE WITH TOLSTOY

To contemplate the prairie is
To fathom time, to guess at infinite space,
To find the Earth-spirit in a dreaming mood.
In Illinois the prairies are a soul,
A Muse of distance eyeing the solitude.
It is not the mountain's soul, the lonely face
Of the desert, nor the canyon's, even though
There is no goal here for the eye but fields,
And levels to the dim horizon's rim.
They are a sea of grass, and they have waves
When the winds sweep over them and shade,
And brighten the fields, and the shadow of the hawk,
The cloud is hurried over miles of grass,
Dotted with barns and houses, long heaped graves
In country yards. Breaking the stillness a cock
May crow afar, and charm the sleeping air,
As white clouds with an ancient mission pass.
Crows may fly over, as the sunlight's glare
Mingles with silence, which the grasshopper
Scarcely disturbs with his somnolent whirr.
But to the north a river's flow is shored
By a drift of hills, enclosing the prairie land;
And over all a blinding light is poured,
In which the banners of the corn unfurl
And breathe and flutter, gathering a store
Of sweetness for the harvest. But above all
Is the spirit of the scene, the mystical
Presence, not wholly nature, and not man,
But made of these, made even of the dead,
Whose living hands reaped here, and who began
With prairie plows to subdue, to cultivate
This vastness, and who met the human fate,
And sank into this earth. They interfuse,
With deity added, these wide voiceless miles

Of meadows, who won the dignity of earth:
Kincaid, McDoel, Ensley, Watkins, Miles,
Houghton and Masters speak here as the Muse
Of this domain, they whisper of toil, of mirth,
Of the gracious days, before the republic grown
With the lust of trade to power imperial,
And battleships to man far distant seas
Of isles and ports, sapped all this fertile realm,
And gnawed to the very bone the substance of
Their sons, to the decay of liberty,
And the scarcity of bread, as tyrannies
Did this, for now is tyranny
Masked as a benefactor. A slow disease,
Fatal, progressive, has ruined the republic's strength.

My grandfather was so typical of the people of Menard County along the Sangamon River that I can describe them as temperaments, as American influences, as exemplars of Americanism by a few touches concerning his life and ways, his political and social faith. He was a Jeffersonian Democrat, and a devoted adherent to the causes of Jackson. His Tennessee nativity may have helped his admiration for Jackson, but it was in his blood to live by the American principles of the Old Warrior, and by the philosophy of the wise man of Monticello. For his father, his father's father and grandfather were born in Virginia. His father hated slavery, and on coming to Illinois in 1829 emancipated his one slave. The deed of emancipation may be read at the courthouse in Livingston, Overton County, Tennessee, to this day.

LEWIS ROSS BUILT A FINE BRICK HOUSE MODELED AFTER ONE HE HAD ADMIRED ON THE BANKS OF THE HUDSON

His nature was a touching blend of simple piety and human love, good will, courage, hopefulness, prudent judgment in the business affairs of farming, industry, fair dealing with everyone. George Kirby, his lifelong neighbor, also of Tennessee blood, was much like him in respect to the virtues of the good neighbor, the just man, though lacking the spiritual vision and urges which my grandfather had.

My grandfather had some of the idealism which we associate with Tolstoy. Like the great Russian, he hated war and believed all war was unnecessary. He hated oppression and cruelty, to human beings or to animals. He was a man of great charity, and abounding generosities and kindnesses. He spent money generously for magnanimous causes and for help to those who were in misfortune. He was opposed, even to impatience at times, to all forms of dishonesty, and falsehood, thriftlessness and drink. As a good neighbor he kept the scales on his farm open freely to all to come and weigh their cattle and hogs without any fee. And he was wont to drive around the neighborhood with apples or peaches for those who did not have them, and to visit those who were old and bedridden. He would never attend the county fair, because he abhorred the drinking and disorder that sometimes occurred on the grounds; particularly was this the case after the time that the drunken driver of a bus ran over a boy and killed him near the grandstand. That settled the fair for him. His words were that he would rather see a dog fight than attend the fair.

In another place I have spoken of him as he appeared at Concord Church; and I might add here that his religion was so simple and tender and loving that the scoffers who knew him used to say that if religion was like that of the Old Squire it was a good thing. But what now comes into my memory is his courtly and gracious manner with his fellows. Often I was with him in the family carriage as he drove about Sandridge. I can hear his voice yet, so kindly, so fraternal as he spoke to people we passed on the way. It would be, "Good mornin', James, good mornin', sir." And I would ask, "Who is that, grandpa?" And he would say, "That is Jimmy Senter," or Sammy Colson, or Jimmy Traylor, or John Wiedeman "who lives over in Dutchland by the river"; or "that is Joe Gordon, poor man, who can't make a livin'."

He could tolerate no kind of vulgarity, or profanity, and never heard it without reproof, except in the case of George Kirby. When horses were bred in the lot he would retire to his living room and read the Petersburg *Observer*. One of his neighbors was Cyrus Hoheimer, a huge, fat, tobacco-chewing fellow. Grandfather did not like Cy's vulgarity, and he detested his use of tobacco. One time Cy came by in a wagon in which a huge sow was being hauled. My grandfather was sitting under the maple trees in the front yard. Cyrus said, "Good mornin', Uncle Squire." The return salutation was "Good mornin', Cyrus, good mornin', sir." Then Cyrus, with tobacco juice running at the corners of his mouth, said, "I'm takin' my sow over to the boar." Grandfather clicked his teeth with "tut, tut" and followed that with "disgusting, disgusting." Then he turned away and went into the house.

I have told in another book, *Across Spoon River,* about his turning back to Seth Thomas the forty acres lost by hiding away when the Civil War was on, deeding it back just on repayment of the taxes and the money he had spent for fences.

His devotion to my grandmother in a marriage that lasted seventy years has few parallels. They used to ride about the Sandridge country together laughing and talking like young lovers, exclaiming about the fields of corn and oats, or the songs of the meadow larks. How they were beloved on Sandridge! How they are remembered with a kind of hushed reverence by the grandchildren of those who knew and loved them! For they gave Sandridge its character, they helped to make the other people like them, a people whose religious adorations were clear and sweet as the fields, and utterly alien to incense and ritual. The sky and the meadows inspired them and their neighbors with a goodness and a worship so simple and beautiful that it hurts the heart to think it was ever lost. I am happy that this was my nurturing spot of earth, as it is still my spiritual home and as they are still my people. Still that prairie country from Petersburg to the Mason County Hills is brooded over by their influence. Their names thrill my heart, as it happened recently when a man approached me in Petersburg and said that his name was Clary, and added, "I knew your grandfather for many years. He was the best man I ever knew." This in a tone of voice that belonged to the Sandridge people.

The distance between New Salem Hill, on the Sangamon, and Lewistown, five miles north of the Spoon River, is something over thirty miles. Lewistown is one of the old towns of Illinois. It was incorporated in 1823, and at one time was the county seat of the county that stretched from the Mississippi to Lake Michigan. Chicago was then a hamlet, and all public business such as the payment of taxes was transacted at Lewistown. The town was named after Lewis Ross, the son of Ossian Ross, who came from New York. Lewis Ross became very distinguished. He was in the Mexican War, he was an Illinois legislator and a member of Congress. He belonged to that devoted set of men who admired Douglas and hoped to see him president, and grieved when the wheel of fortune took all his hopes away. He built at Lewistown a fine brick house modeled after one he had admired on the banks of the Hudson. For many years he dispensed a gracious hospitality at this Lewistown mansion. My grandfather and grandmother were wont to drive from Sandridge to pay visits to him and his Virginia wife. He had a relative named Harvey Ross who at one time carried the mail by horseback from Springfield to Lewistown, passing through New Salem, where Lincoln was the postmaster in 1833. Lincoln received the appointment under the administration of Jackson, with whom he was not in sympathy and whose policies he opposed. As the New Salem post office was of no great moment, the appointment was suffered to stand.

Havana, on the Illinois River at its confluence with the Spoon, was fathered by Ossian Ross, who for many years ran a hotel there and managed the ferry which carried traffic to Fulton County and on the way to Lewistown. Across the Illinois at Havana there are the Spoon River bottoms, a place of giant weeds, huge elms and oaks, tangled vines, and swamps fed by the seep of the river and the lowlands. Passing up the Spoon River country one comes to Duncan's Mills, where there was a covered bridge when I was a boy, a store or two, a few houses. Here was once one of the first gristmills of the region. Ten miles farther along is Bernadotte, where also there was a gristmill when as a young man I used to ride about that country with Dr. Strode, the naturalist. This is a region of hills and oak woods on the heights and was always noted for its lawless roughs, who got into the courts for assaults and murders. At New Salem there were wrestling matches, horse races, foot races, and at times fist fights. But these men were a different breed from the Spoon River crowd. They were more laughing, humorous, and more given to hospitality and amiable delights. There is a beauty about Bernadotte, and farther up the river at Ellisville, but after all the country is not the prairie. And so the Spoon River may be traced north and east past the place where it takes in Big Creek, until it fades away beyond Knox County, where the Swedes became predominant at Galesburg. That is a different country, as alien to New Salem and Sandridge as are the Ozarks.

TEN MILES FURTHER ALONG IS BERNADOTTE,

WHERE ALSO THERE WAS A GRISTMILL

CHAPTER THREE

FRANCIS PARKMAN (1823-1893), despite ill-health and partial blindness, knew the Illinois country along the Kankakee and Illinois rivers. He saw Starved Rock, and the site of the great Illinois town of the Indians. In his working day he saw the corrupting approach of the merchant philosophy, and with intrepid courage and vast industry devoted himself to the task of saving the republic. In that wise and invaluable book by Van Wyck Brooks, *New England: Indian Summer,* there is a well-deserved tribute to this heroic man, who wrote books not much read at the time, like *The Conspiracy of Pontiac*, whose war had much to do with the history of the continent. Parkman admired the Indians out of a courage and an endurance which made him kin to them. He lived during the time of Shickshack, the Menard County Indian who befriended the whites, and who at death was given burial in a great hill not far from Chandlerville and the Sangamon River, in the west part of the county. Shabbona was an Illinois Indian chief born in a village on the Kankakee River. He lived until 1859, dying at the age of eighty-four. He, too, befriended the whites, for which he was given land near Shabbona Grove. He went west for a short time, and while he was gone his land was forfeited. Then the citizens of Ottawa raised money and bought him a tract on the Illinois River, near Seneca in Grundy County, and built him a house in which he spent the rest of his life. Like Black Hawk, he was badly treated. These remnants of the first Americans of the Stone Age deserved that civilized consideration which Francis Parkman gave them in his book on the travels of La Salle through the Illinois country. Parkman called La Salle "the pioneer of western pioneers . . . a man of thought trained amid arts and letters." As late as the time of New Salem tribes of Indians came to the Sangamon River bottoms to hunt and to gather the pecans and persimmons in which the woods abounded. But after 1833 Indians were scarce in this country. My grandmother Masters (1814-1910) told me that occasionally in the 1850's an Indian called at the Masters farmhouse asking for food. They had become beggars after once being the owners of the whole domain.

The Black Hawk region is much north of the Sangamon River country and is not in the Illinois River valley, a term that describes that river and the Sangamon and Spoon rivers which flow into it. Black Hawk was defeated in the war that was made upon him in the Rock River country. It is there that a colossal statue was raised to him, later to be described. He was a character that appeals to me, the story of his life and tragedy considered. So it was that I wrote the following poem about him, to be found in my book *More People:*

BLACK HAWK

This is the spot where Black Hawk, fully dressed
In the uniform that Andrew Jackson gave,
Was buried upright, this is that West
Which cured at last his wrong, his heart's unrest,
The wound of loneliness in his hawk-like breast,
This spot is Black Hawk's grave.

His body became a fellow to the rain,
And prairie winds. They buried him with his hand
Upon the cane which Henry Clay
Had given him in a better day,
Before he lost his land.
They placed his hand upon that cane,

Perhaps to signify his weak command,
His need of guidance and support
When soldiers from the Chesapeake,
From the Chicago Fort
Hastened to Ogle County and Bad Axe Creek.

In death they placed his hand upon
That walking stick, as symbol, it may be,
As if to say 'twas possible to free
His people, and that he might have won
By guidance the land whereof his tribe was shorn,
The hunting grounds, whose loss brought poverty.
In life he had not any staff,
In life his life was overborne
By slaughter and the need of corn—
This is the Indian's, this the world's sole epitaph.

He had returned from Iowa, thereby
Breaking his word not ever to return,
But forced by hunger and the need of corn
To seek his land and village in Illinois,
From which he had been driven. Then the cry
Of Illinois was raised, and fears destroy
Justice and mercy, and breed all cruelty.
And there at Stillman's Run
Some eighteen hundred scared militiamen
Gathered in hate with sword and gun,
With whisky and with food,
Against three hundred starving Reds.
And there they slew emerging from a wood
Three Indian trucemen, bearing a flag of truce.
Such was their cowardice, their dreads,
Such the reception to the Message men,
Striving to say Black Hawk had come again

To Illinois for corn, not battle, or to abuse
The peace of White man. These three paid the price
Of drunkenness and craven cowardice,
Emerging with a white flag from the trees,
Unarmed and asking peace.

Then Black Hawk went to war!
As a wounded eagle on the hunter swoops
He raised the battle cry, and in courage stood
At Bad Axe River, meeting General Scott
With Federal soldiers, who soon was conqueror
Of Black Hawk and his scarce four hundred troops,
His hungry, gaunt, woe-stricken band,
His old men, women, children, ponies caught
In this trap by the losing of his land.

So Black Hawk made a prisoner
Was taken in chains on a triumphal tour
Over America, to show him the mighty stir
Of the White man in the cities,
To show him the cities magnificent, secure,
Springing like blossoms from the Indian land;
To show him the unconquerable American cities,
Where neither justice was, nor pities,
To show him how the Indian could not stand
Against the White man—it could be no more.

At last they turned him loose. And he came back
To Illinois and looked upon the wreck
Of his native village. With tears he passed the site
Of his wasted hearth. His cheeks ran down with tears
For happy days now past, his ruined home,
Crushed by the ruthless White.
He wandered then for years

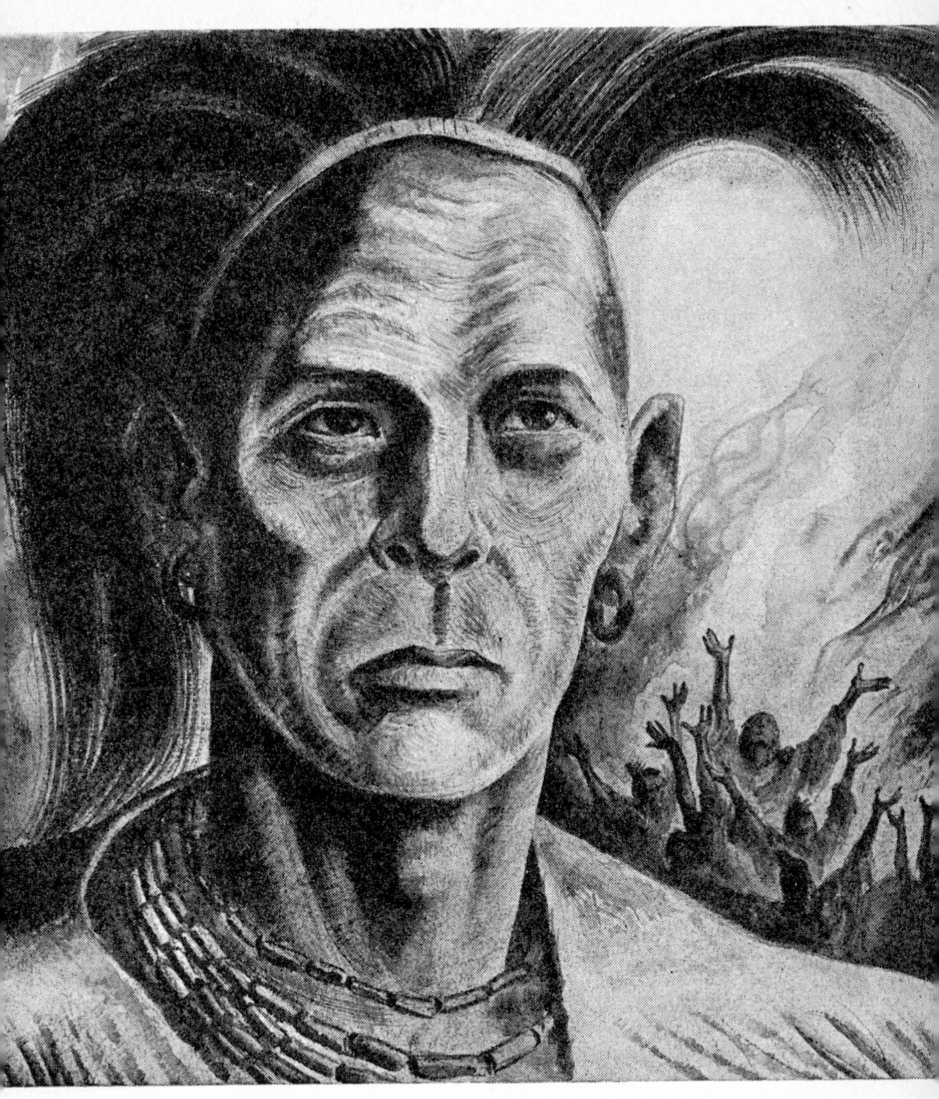

BLACK HAWK WAS DEFEATED IN THE WAR THAT WAS MADE UPON HIM IN THE ROCK RIVER COUNTRY

Back and forth, back and forth
From Iowa to Illinois, south and north,
East and west,
Trying to ease the pain in his breast,
While Illinois shot up with spire and dome,
Dreaming a glorious goal;
While melancholy settled on his soul,
Facing the fate that nothing could revoke,
Facing it as he aged, facing it dumb—
He could not speak out of a heart that broke.

He died and was given burial
Where winds on the prairie wail.
They gave his body to the snow and rain,
Sitting erect in a deep-spaded grave;
They placed his hand upon that cane,
The gift of Henry Clay,
Who tried to guide, to save
America in his day.

The White men had Chief Black Hawk's land;
But with the years it wasted, thinned,
It blew away like sand,
It mounted the wings of the wind,
Leaving the once rich fields
To the gulch, the gully, and the dusty ditch
Where earth had been so rich,
Because of the grass's roots,
The tendrils, undershoots
Which held the soil, and loosed it being gone.
And every ten years the White man for a whim
Went further West, moved on,
Like locusts, to consume
Fresh land, fresh land to skim—

These Whites, too, had their doom.
For as they starved Chief Black Hawk, so they killed
The land they took, they wrought despairs
To the homesites of future men,
Of the land the rightful heirs.
They did not fertilize as they tilled;
They left the glacial soil
Without protection to be washed by rain,
Growing less fruitful to any toil.
They scooped the strip-mines, leaving deep ravines,
Where once the banners of the corn unfurled
While cities shot up to the sky, the world
Became their province, conquered by machines.

The jungle waits the cities with intercrossed
Branches of vines on a land that is lost,
First lost to Black Hawk, then to us,
Whose faith has been forsworn
Through years calamitous—
The White man now needs corn.

CHAPTER FOUR

THE MOST beautiful, as well as the most historic, part of the Sangamon River is in Menard County, along the boundary of New Salem village and at Petersburg. Illinois was first divided into counties of large areas. But as Illinois grew populous from immigration from the East, and from the South coming through Shawneetown on the Ohio River, some of the large counties were split to make other political subdivisions. It was so with Menard County, which was formed by striking off 198,000 acres from Sangamon County. Until 1824 the boundaries of Sangamon County contained many other counties, such as McLean, which is very large, and Menard, which is one of the smallest counties in the state. It was at the session of the legislature of 1838-1839 that Menard County was created out of Sangamon County territory. This new county was named after Pierre Menard, a Frenchman, who was born in Quebec in 1767. La Salle and his fellow Frenchman had done much to attract French settlers to Illinois. In the northern part of the state are many towns of French names, and the descendants of French blood.

Pierre Menard stayed in Quebec until his nineteenth year when he came to the Illinois country, embarking as a merchant at Vincennes. Later, in 1790, he formed a business partnership with a merchant named DuBois, and their stock of goods was moved to Kaskaskia on the Mississippi River. Menard stands in history as a candid and honest man, whose industry and good judgment brought him to fortune. He was a member of the Illinois Legislative Council before Illinois was a state, as well as president of that body. He was made lieutenant governor when Illinois entered the Union in 1818.

Kaskaskia was founded in 1703 as a Roman Catholic mission, four years after Cahokia, which is the oldest town in Illinois. Kaskaskia became the first capital of Illinois. The town was built around a park-like square on which stood the buildings of the Jesuits.

On narrow streets that radiated from the square were log houses with roofs of thatch or bark. There was stone in the near-by bluffs with which the better class of residents built their houses. There were plenty of fine furnishings here, such as gilt-framed mirrors, paintings and billiard tables. Kaskaskia lost ground owing to the wars and British rule. But in 1809 it received fresh life by being made the capital of Illinois Territory, and the regional land office. In 1818 it became the capital of the state, but lost the honor in 1820 when the seat of government was moved to Vandalia. Floods from the Mississippi hastened the decline of Kaskaskia, and near the end of the nineteenth century the Mississippi overflowed the peninsula which separated it from the Kaskaskia River, changing its course and obliterating the old town. Now there is Kaskaskia Island between the new and the old channel of the river, and the modern community receives its mail from St. Mary's, Missouri.

Yet the Pierre Menard house still stands, a story and a half structure with a hip roof and dormer windows, looking something like the plantation houses of Louisiana. It was built in 1802, and for that day was a splendid affair. The foundation is of stone blocks. The frame is of hewn timbers a foot square. Later some of the original furnishings were authenticated and placed in the mansion by the state. Pierre Menard became a rich man, and much admired for his ability and his generous attitude toward his fel-

MENARD STANDS IN HISTORY AS A CANDID AND HONEST MAN, WHOSE INDUSTRY AND GOOD JUDGMENT BROUGHT HIM TO FORTUNE

lows and the Indians. There is documentary proof to show that in 1820, while he was an agent in the Indian Department, he spent $13 to have a Delaware chief and his party ferried across the Mississippi, besides $19.50 to give supper and breakfast to thirteen Indians and for feed for their horses, and $23 to buy 400 pounds of beef and have a coffin made for an Indian who had been accidentally killed. In this house Lafayette was entertained in 1824, where he received visitors in a room that still contains a mantelpiece imported from France.

Behind the house is a stone kitchen with an enormous fire place and a Dutch oven, and a sink carved from a large block of stone. Near by is the old slave house, which has been carefully restored. A slope runs to the river from the house and at its base is the site of Old Kaskaskia over which the waters of the Mississippi flow. This is the man for whom Menard County was named. He died in 1844 when New Salem village was gone back to the minks and the rabbits, and all its buildings were in ruins or moved away to the new town of Petersburg, two miles down the Sangamon.

Menard County was organized on the plan of precincts, while many counties of the state have what is known as township organization. New Salem was in Sangamon County at the time it was platted. With the organization of Menard County it fell within the boundaries of the Petersburg precinct.

The Sangamon River occupies about 700 acres within the boundaries of the county. The country along its shores for a mile or two back is hilly and broken, and covered with heavy timber; then the undulating expanses of the prairie begin and stretch in every direction dotted by groves of trees. Irish Grove, Bee Grove and Sugar Grove all have great trees made up of black, spotted, burr, white and pin oak; and by elm, ash, walnut, hard and soft maples, sycamore, linden, hickory of several varieties, cottonwood, black and honey locust, pecan, cherry and mulberry. Nothing is more grateful to the eye than to turn from the levels of grass to these groves of trees which break the monotony of the prairie. Little Grove and Clary's Grove are on the west side of the river, the latter about four miles from New Salem. Menard County has boasted for a century that it contains the finest body of land in the world. That the soil is exceedingly fertile, that there is coal under the soil and fine timber on top of the soil cannot be disputed, and that corn, oats, wheat grow there in abundance is equally true.

After the admission of Illinois into the Union, immigration began to flow into the Sangamon River country. The Kellys located in Springfield, coming from North Carolina in 1818. The Clarys, including John Clary, who was notable at New Salem, came from Tennessee in 1819, and took up their residence at what became known as Clary's Grove. Some of the

BY THIS TIME, NEW SALEM WAS A DESERTED

'ILLAGE: EVERYONE BUT JACK KELSO WAS GONE

names of the first settlers of Menard County may be listed to indicate what truly American stocks peopled it. They were the Armstrongs, the Goodpastures, the Engles, Smoots, Kings, Atterberrys, Bells, Watkinses. Lounsberrys, Pantiers, McDoels, Hudspeths, Onstotts, Estills, Alkires, Greens, Cogdells, Kincaids, Combs', Hoheimers, Battertons, Bales, Elmores, Kirbys, Shorts, Berrys, Reavises, Blaines, Spearses, and many more, all from the South, all of English, Irish and Scotch-Irish blood.

Menard County has a number of villages, but most of them can be covered quickly. Athens is near the Sangamon River, and sprang up shortly after the survey of New Salem; that is, soon after 1829. Tallula and Greenview were founded in 1857, and there is little to say of them. The latter was named for William G. Greene, who ran a store at New Salem and became the richest man of the county, and a man of political influence owing to his association with Lincoln. His residence and great farm were near Tallula, near Clary's Grove, and not far from New Salem where he lived after his days in the village on the Hill until the turn of the century.

A great deal can be said about Petersburg. In New Salem was George Warburton, who erected the second store in that village, and also Peter Lukins, the shoemaker. These two owned much of the land on which Petersburg was built, as well as land around the site. In the fall of 1832 Warburton laid out a town, perhaps in anticipation of the decline of New Salem. In the fall of the same year Peter Lukins acquired the quarter section of land on which the original Petersburg was laid out. At this time Lukins was running a tavern in the south part of the place and following his trade of making shoes. The question arose between these two landowners as to the name to be given to the new town. They settled it by playing a game of seven-up. If Warburton won the game, the town should be called Georgetown; if Peter Lukins won, the town should be called Petersburg. Lukins won the game and Petersburg it was.

There was plenty of drinking in that country. There was nothing in life lived in that fresh air to produce ragged nerves, but I can see how men got bored, how they enjoyed the lift of a drink. Both Warburton and Lukins drank to excess. One morning after Lukins had been on a drunk he was found dead in bed. And one morning Warburton's body was found in the Sangamon River, face down in six inches of water. Some believed that he had committed suicide; some thought that he had fallen into the water in a drunken stupor. In either case one of the founders of Petersburg had made his exit. Before that he had sold his interest in the Petersburg site to Hezekiah King of St. Louis, who had the place replatted by Lincoln, who was lingering at New Salem. The plat was acknowledged before Justice Bowling

Green, still living in his old house up the Springfield road about a mile away. This was in 1836.

The country was stirring with excitement about slavery and the attitude of Mexico, with which country war was only ten years ahead. There were thirteen million people in the United States, and men were moving around to get land; they were hurrying to Illinois, to that part of Sangamon County which became Menard County, with Petersburg for the county seat. So now Petersburg was soon the home of the Wrights, Lanings, Bennetts, McNeelys, among the better known names. And Petersburg grew. The flats from the foot of the hills to the Sangamon River were well adapted to a square and for the business part of the town. The hills were beautiful sites for residences, and these were quickly built, some of brick, like the house of Robert Bishop, the gunsmith, and like the Gault house.

Standing on that hill where John Brahm, the banker, built his house, the tops of the trees in the courthouse yard and the dome of the courthouse are slightly below the spectator, with the Sangamon River in view farther east. One can sweep his eyes around from the hill, where Major Harris of Mexican War fame had his residence, on south along the river to Wolf Fuelner's brewery, and then around to the hill where the Catholic church was built, and then west still along the hill where many fine houses were built along the years. The prospect is an amphitheater. Petersburg is one of the most attractive towns in Illinois, and has always been noted for its enterprise, its good architecture on the square and on the hills, and for its genial and happy societies. I believe there is and always has been less of village spite in Petersburg than in any town that I know about. Local dramatic companies were always springing up, playing *Pinafore* and the like. It built a good opera house, it organized a military company, it had the circus crowd later to be noticed. It thwarted prohibition, almost as well as Havana did in Mason County. The farmers on Saturday thronged Luthinger's restaurant. There were parties and dances and private poker clubs, and the breeding of race horses all about, and as far away as Oakford; and there was the Menard County Fair.

A few words here may be interpolated about hamlets like Oakford and Atterberry located in the beautiful prairie country of Sandridge Precinct. These came along much later than Athens and Petersburg, and have slept along the years as the river twisted its way to the Illinois. There is also Robinson's Mills, which came to be known as Bobtown. It nestled among the hills of the northwest part of the county, in a vicinity supposed to be adapted to the culture of grapes and the manufacture of wines. But Bobtown faded out, for nothing much came of such hopes. An attempt was made to found a town named Huron in the north part of the county on the river, but it came to nothing. And truly this territory, as the river reaches the western boundary of the county where it touches Mason County, is anything but attractive. The river is rather forbidding, as it flows through lonely forests of sycamores and elms, or passes by poor uplands and sand hills. Here river birds flit through the sky and crows fly to their nests in the woods, and the silence and the sunlight reign, or the eternal clouds drift from the west over what never became Huron, over the pathetic emptiness of Bobtown. Yet, as a boy, Bobtown was a thing of wonder to me. It was somewhere at the seam of the sky and the earth, it was a place where there was a wagon shop, where an anvil rang all day long, where there was a store in which candy and chewing gum wrapped in colored tissue paper, and scented with cinnamon, could be bought.

And to think that New Market, Miller's Ferry, Huron presumed to contest with Petersburg for the county-seatship. That was decided in 1839, and soon Petersburg had a jail and a courthouse, and the town began to grow. Like the county itself, it was peopled from the South, though there were some families from New Jersey and New York. By this time New Salem was a deserted village, everyone but Jack Kelso was gone. He still lived on the New Salem Hill amid the oaks, he still walked into Petersburg bringing fish from the Sangamon to sell. The Rutledge Tavern was leaning and falling, the grass was creeping from the prairie at the west and obliterating paths, and spaces where games were played. The Onstott coopershop had been moved bodily to Petersburg and set up again. One log house had been brought and reconstructed back of old Robert Bishop's gunsmith shop on the square. Yes, and it must be mentioned that Robert Bishop was not from the South, he was one of the exceptions as to nativity. He was born in Portsmouth, England, and came with his parents to Boston where he was reared and schooled. He spent ten years of his early life as a whaler on the Atlantic, along the coast of Chile, Peru and Panama. How did he get to Petersburg? It was from St. Louis, where he had gone to follow his trade as a gunsmith. He may have heard of the hunters of Menard along the Sangamon. At any rate, he got to Menard County in 1841, built a good brick house on the side of one of the hills of Petersburg, which still stands, went to the Mexican War with a considerable contingent of Menard men, then returned to Petersburg and went on keeping the gunshop with his sons Jay and Wheeler. Only a year or so ago Jay lost his life, in his late seventies, through the collapse of the old outhouse in the yard which precipitated him into the pit where he was suffocated. That may be a symbol of what many little towns do to weary citizens who walk the square and pine for larger life, or different life. Old Robert Bishop is still vivid in my memory, his black eyes and gray beard and hair, his deep, sleepy voice as he talked to the hunters about their guns, as I stood by full of wonder, having entered the store after a long look at the pistols, bullet molds, old swords, slingshots, ancient pictures of ships, which could be seen in his show window from the sidewalk. Always I had to walk through the store to the rear where I could see the log building that had once stood on the New Salem Hill. I could not resist celebrating the death of Jay Bishop, having no malice in heart at all, as he had none toward anyone. For many years he walked the Petersburg square, whittling and talking, for years after his father and mother were dead, and his brother Wheeler was dead. Jay never married, and so the family is now extinct, unless Wheeler married.

CHAPTER FIVE

I KNOW of no town in Illinois more attractive than Petersburg on the Sangamon. It was largely populated by Kentuckians. The square looks to the east of hills, and to the north of hills, and likewise to the south of hills. The very old houses are on the slopes and some of them right down to the square. The mansions are on the hills all around, and some of them are very good, and of excellent architecture, for men like N. W. Branson, the leading lawyer until his death thirty years ago, and Thompson W. Mc-

Neely, a congressman in his day, became prosperous and built themselves good homes, and even fine homes considering the size of Petersburg, though none so commodious and handsome as the house of Lewis W. Ross at Lewistown in the Spoon River country.

Across the river to the east, reached by a covered bridge in my boyhood, was the brewery of Wolf Fuelner, for a population such as Petersburg and the surrounding country had, made up of Kentuckians, Tennesseans, and after 1848 added to by Germans coming up by way of New Orleans and Alton, could not dispense with beer and whisky. To the north of the town on a hill was a vineyard and a winery. In going out of Petersburg to the north and the west hills must be climbed on the way to Sandridge and Tallula. But it is not so in traveling to Springfield. In that direction the road runs by the river beneath the hills and slopes crowned with oaks, past the spot where until recently stood the Charter Oak Mill, once owned by Captain Wright, of Mexican War fame, a man much devoted to Douglas. Another devoted admirer that Douglas had at Petersburg was Major Thomas Harris, whose name will be found in all the books about Douglas and Lincoln. His house was on the hill near the winery. The Bennetts and Raineys of Virginia, the Bales and Montgomerys of Kentucky were among those who gave a quality to Petersburg, not to mention John A.

Brahm whose mother was from Virginia. He was the banker and the richest man in Petersburg, until the speculations of a son-in-law brought him to poverty dire and ignominious.

In the days of his prosperity he walked about town with straight shoulders and outthrust abdomen, confident and self-satisfied, displaying a large watch charm, and proud perhaps that he had begun to accumulate his fortune by selling onions raised on his father's farm on Sandridge. He had built the stone-faced bank on the square with its marble columns, and the large store on the corner, always called "the broad-gauge," and a very fine store it was, finished inside in walnut, with counters of walnut, and shelves back of them on which were goods not surpassed in quality and variety in the stores in Springfield. Everything he did was of the best. Then he lost all, including the interest of the people. As he declined in health he walked about the square borrowing a quarter from unwilling people whom he had befriended in the days of his prosperity. His sons did not turn out well. One died a drunkard, the other became a clog dancer and banjo player, who boasted of his father's relationship to Brahms, the composer. Such was John Brahm, who for long years was a partner of William G. Greene in the banking business there in Petersburg, after Greene had taken up his residence near Tallula, and left long behind him New Salem and his days as collector of internal revenue in the Lincoln administration. John Brahm lay in an unmarked grave in Oakland until Harmon Marbold, a rich German farmer who lived east and north of Petersburg, near Greenview, raised the necessary money to give him a stone.

There were many Germans in Menard County, on Sandridge and elsewhere, and many in Petersburg. Luthinger's bakery restaurant and beer saloon on the corner of the square was their place of resort. Luthinger came from Alsace-Lorraine. Marbold was from Hanover, and after service as a hired farm hand he became a landowner near the village of Sweetwater. He was the chief man perhaps of those Germans in Menard County, and perhaps the richest of all of them. They went to Germany with the cattle they had sold, and returned with wine from the Rhine. They seemed to give a liberal quality to Petersburg, making it very different from the Puritan Lewistown thirty miles or so north.

It is ironic that, in this town and county of opposition to the War Between the States, B. F. Stephenson (1827-1874), who founded the Grand Army of the Republic, was buried in Rose Hill, the very beautiful cemetery over the hill from Wolf Fuelner's brewery. But for that matter Petersburg, which furnished many soldiers for the war, and before that for the fight on Mexico, organized a militia company in 1877 and named it after Major Harris—the Harris Guards, it was. When this company marched forth to cow strikers in the coal regions Petersburg looked on in wonder and fear. In the rank and file of this company were Germans like Albert Oeltjen and Leo Werner, and Jews like Julius Rothschild and Leopold Ahronheim, besides a son of Major Harris, some of the Hatfields, Raineys and Wrights. Petersburg had many Jewish families, the Rothschilds, Nusbaums, Katzensteins, Lilienthals, Hainsfeathers, Kahns and others. They were as much a part of the town as any of the Gentiles, with whom they mingled, by whom they were patronized and elected to office without any discrimination. And this was long ago.

Petersburg made no use of the Sangamon River, for there was little that could be done with it. There are beautiful hills on the east side of the river at Petersburg, hills that melt into rich uplands. The left side of the river is flat land, extending all the way west to the hills of the residential part of the town. In times of flood the river overflows this part of Petersburg. Once when I lived there as a boy the river spread to the very square and men were doing errands and going here and there in rowboats. At this time, and at other times like it, the health of the city was menaced with various contagious diseases.

Through Petersburg the river crawls in a general northerly direction, toward Sandridge and Mason County. It was New Salem that put the river to use. There was the Camron and Rutledge Mill, which was torn down in 1841 when New Salem was completely abandoned. The second mill, which was in the same place and altogether larger and better constructed than the first one, was destroyed by fire in December of 1883. That left the dam to fall into decay, for no other mill has been built. In the restoration of New Salem it is planned to build another mill, but as yet it has not been done.

The river at Petersburg has been used by fishermen, though not much. We used to swim and wade near the covered bridge that spanned the river. But most of us were afraid of the suckholes and currents that rumor had the river full of, and most of us, though native to the river, were not good swimmers. In the hot months it was customary for gangs to walk to the bridge and take a dip in the yellow water.

The flats on the Petersburg side of the river were used by the circuses which visited the town every season, like Sells Brothers and Burr Robbins and Ringling Brothers, before that circus became the monstrous organization which it was later. What fun to see the circus come to town, to see the tents laid out and the stakes distributed, to see John Walker, the butcher, bring beef to the lions, to see hay delivered to the elephants, to peek into the dining tent and the dressing tent, and satisfy our curiosity about the clowns and performers before we saw them under the white top! My father had his law office at first in the old courthouse, the one where the first dignitaries, like Lincoln and others, argued causes, where

Herndon appeared, often tipsy, and amused the spectators. After a time Father had an office in one of the attractive buildings on the west side of the square, and here I used to sit in a window and watch the circus parades.

Petersburg produced a number of circus performers, and later it became the home of a winter circus. There was first Harry Lambkin, an equilibrist. Later there were the Bennett boys, who began their careers as tumblers and bareback riders by practicing in barns about town. Then there was Ed Shipp, who belonged to one of the early families of Petersburg. He became ring master for Ringling Brothers, Barnum and Bailey's, and later still owned a circus which toured South America, and went broke there a few years ago. Before that he built an octagonal structure in Petersburg for his winter circus, in which his clowns and performers appeared. The winter circus was one of the delights of the town until quite recently. The circus crowd spending the winter in Petersburg added excitement to the place. In my boyhood Harry Lambkin, a half brother of Shipp, had a gymnasium over Fisher's drugstore on the corner, equipped with horizontal bars, trapezes and mats, and boxing gloves. To build up my somewhat frail physique my father put me in this gymnasium one winter where I learned all I ever knew of boxing, which was not much.

I marvel to this day at the activity of Petersburg,

AFTER A TIME, MY FATHER HAD AN OFFICE ON

THE WEST SIDE OF THE SQUARE IN PETERSBURG

at the genial-natured, high-minded character of the leading people there, like the Lanings, the Wrights, the Brahms, the McNeelys. They proved their blood in such cases as Harris Laning the son of C. B. Laning, a partner in the "broad-gauge store," who became a rear admiral in the navy, and like Edward Laning, the grandson of the excellent lawyer of that name, who has made a place for himself as an artist. Perhaps the finest house still in Petersburg is that of the elder Edward Laning, all of pressed brick and Victorian towers and balconies, standing in picturesque view at the foot of the hill which one passes going out of town toward Tallula.

Petersburg had a baseball nine, a very formidable set of players, the time and place considered. The pitcher was Powell Antle, who was the admiration and the wonder of us boys, who used to sit on the grass and watch him throw a curve ball, a miracle thing in those days of the eighties. He was a college man, and became a physician. Of all cases of disappearances his was the most mysterious that I know about. He was happily married, he had an adored son, he was prosperous, happily domiciled in a fine house that his prosperous father had built him. And one night he walked out of his house after the evening meal and was never seen or heard of again. They explored the old coal mines near town to see if he had fallen in one of them, they dragged the Sangamon River, they searched the country, and offered rewards for news of him. Nothing came of all this. He had vanished, as if snatched up by some supermundane power that the late Charles Fort wrote about.

Then one winter Petersburg organized a company to play *Pinafore,* in which the laughing Theodore Fisher took the part of Sir Joseph, while Kate Degge sang Josephine, and did it so well that she was offered a part in a professional company. Her pious family refused to let her leave home. My father impersonated Dick Deadeye, and my mother Little Buttercup, and lovely Mrs. "Buck" Wright lent charm to the character of Cousin Phoebe. The opera was given in what was known as Fisher's Hall, a small affair used by traveling theatricals before the Harris Guards' Opera House was built, a very good structure just west of the square. Along the way Rule's Livery Stable had a stage, on which one time Haverly's Minstrels gave a performance. They were stranded in Petersburg, and to make the best of it they offered to give a city program right in this little town; for a hundred dollars, I believe it was. Petersburg promptly raised the money, according to its usual enterprising way of doing things. That's what the Kentucky and Virginia blood did for this town.

The country about was a place for raising race horses. The Watkinses living all about near Petersburg, such as "Redhead" Sammy Watkins, and the Watkinses near Oakford bred quarter-horses and racers of all sorts, which performed at the Menard County Fair, an annual event, while the fairs of other counties near by dropped and gave up. The Menard County Fair was an event of much excitement for the country people, and for the circus crowd so far as they remained in Petersburg during the summer. And there were fights among the Bennetts, for one of them was Jack Bennett, a handy man with a brick, and one fighter was Knowlt McHenry, who weighed about 125 pounds, but of whom everyone was afraid. There were also the Hoheimer boys, who fought with knives and bricks. All the while my father was the state's attorney and lived unharmed, though he prosecuted without any favor barn burners and the bad men who mutilated cattle.

The fairgrounds were to the north of town on the way to Sandridge. The road fogged with summer dust, and the people in the grandstand sat amid clouds of powdered earth, which floated from the trampled grass and the highway outside. Yes, and there was betting and there were beer stands, such as that run by John Scott, the portly saloon man of Petersburg, patronized liberally by such livers as "Porky" Jim Thomas of Oakford and the Germans of Dutchland north of Sandridge.

There was a flavor of Virginia and Kentucky in all this. William Greene of Tallula always attended the fairs to see the races and to walk about the grounds with old friends. One could see John Brahm, in all his stately manner, moving about among the people, smiling in his friendly way on everyone. He was truly a man of great public spirit and great kindness.

Not far from the fairgrounds, just where the road turns north after running west from the Estill hill, stood the brick house of James Miles, whom I remember for his broad smile and his Sunday dinners when I went there with my grandfather and grandmother. In these days his father George was living, a man born in Maryland in 1796. In my boyhood he was very old. He had a daughter named Anna, who was courted by William H. Herndon when my father was about fifteen. Herndon used to come from the Miles house to the Masters farmhouse, five miles north, for Sunday dinner, bringing Anna, a beautiful woman, as anyone could see from her daguerreotype, which my grandmother kept among her precious trinkets in a drawer of her chest. In this way my father became acquainted with Herndon; later, when my father was state's attorney, he and Herndon practiced law together. He was frequently in Petersburg consulting with my father about cases in the law office on the west side of the square, and on the grass under the shadow of the old historic courthouse.

In these days New Salem was nothing but the water mill at the foot of the hill. The buildings of the village were all gone, save a few logs of the Rutledge Tavern. We knew, we boys, that Lincoln had been postmaster there, but at that time Petersburg was not so friendly to the name of Lincoln as it became later, and as it is today. Just the same, it was great fun to go fishing from the dam, and to wander over the top of the hill which had become a pasture again, joining the limitless prairie to the west.

One time we made up a party to go fishing at New Salem. Herndon was of the party and Theodore Bennett, the circuit clerk, and "Nigger Dick," the comical man of all work, and some others, not remembered, were with us, going in a carriage from Shepherd's livery along the road that led to Springfield. This day the mill was not running. If it had been I should not be telling this story.

My father and Herndon were fishing from the shore north of the mill, while I was climbing about the dam or standing on it to cast my hook for catfish. The mill was between me and Herndon and my father; though when I got on the dam they could see me, and my father kept calling to me to be careful, particularly when I clambered down the logs of the dam to loose my hook. At last I wanted to take a short cut to the dam from the shore. The millrace was between me and the dam, but I did not know it was the millrace, or for that matter what a millrace was. It was a still body of water boarded in, and not more than six feet across, but it was very deep, twenty feet or more. So I stepped in to go to the dam, and down I went, seeing depths of sand-colored water. I knew that I was drowning, and I struggled with regret that I was going to miss the Fourth of July, which was a few days off. Down I went for the second time, and then up but with fading breath. As I went down for the third time Jim Arnold, a cross-eyed youth, reached from the shore and grabbed me by my long hair, and held me up to breathe.

Herndon and my father came running around from the north side of the mill, and helped to roll me on the ground to empty my lungs of the water which I had taken in, while my father said, "I told you to be careful," and Herndon laughed. Driving back to Petersburg I was pretty subdued, while Herndon talked on about things that I wish I could remember. So it was that I saw Herndon frequently. He and my father lounged on the grass of the courthouse yard, where Herndon talked of Lincoln and told stories grave and obscene, while my father laughed. This I remember. The stories which Herndon told came to me years later when my father grew reminiscent about his friend, whose mind he pronounced the best that he had ever known.

Perhaps Mentor Graham goes down in American annals as one of its most memorable schoolteachers. He is in all the books on Lincoln, and one of Lindsay's last poems was about him. For fifty years he was a teacher of country schools in Menard County. He was born in Greensburg, Kentucky, in 1800 and died at Black, South Dakota, at a very advanced age.

PERHAPS MENTOR GRAHAM GOES DOWN IN AMERICAN ANNALS AS ONE OF ITS MOST MEMORABLE SCHOOL TEACHERS

When I was a boy in Petersburg he was about the streets, a testy and irritable old man, pragmatic and "grammatical" to the last. He was much in the courts, suing or being sued. Before my day, on one occasion he was sued by Mrs. Bowling Green, the widow of the justice of the peace at New Salem. Another time in a suit in which his son was involved he convulsed the courtroom by his snappy answers to questions and by his visible distaste for the proceedings. He was the subject of practical jokes. My father, who was full of pranks, lowered a tin bug in front of his face, standing behind him. He struck at the bug and my father lifted it, then lowered it again when Graham again struck at it. He finally said querulously, "Did any of you by possibility notice a bug in front of my face?" So he was precise to the end. I saw him many times trotting about the square, but as to how he looked I know as much as I do about the appearance of Perneb. He had two houses in Petersburg, one about a block west of the square, which is still standing, and one near the Alton railroad.

The Menard House on the east side of the square was owned and managed for many years by Jacob Hofing, who came to Petersburg from Hanover, Germany. This was the popular and very well-conducted hotel of the town, where the lawyers stopped who traveled the Eighth Circuit, a huge division of Illinois, about 150 miles square. They traveled from Peoria and Pekin on the Illinois River to Metamora in

Woodford County, to Tremont in Tazewell County, to Havana on the Illinois River, to Petersburg and Decatur on the Sangamon River, and on occasion they went to Lewistown near the Spoon River, and tried cases in the historic Courthouse built by Major Walker in 1837. The number of distinguished men who fulmined in this forum is too long to recount. It included such lawyers as O. H. Browning, whose name means nothing now, and Robert G. Ingersoll, still remembered, and Lewis W. Ross, a very considerable barrister in his day. Between the large columns which supported the projecting porch Douglas addressed the people, as Lincoln did.

The upper room of the Menard House was large, and often accommodated the twenty-three members of the grand jury. They retired there to talk till sleep took them, having spent the evening in the office of the hotel where they were regaled by the lawyers with stories, and by William Engle one of the wags of the Greenview neighborhood. Someday I may write a poem of some length about the lawyers who followed the Circuit. It is a theme as rich as that of the Canterbury Pilgrims who started from the Tabbard Inn in Southwark to do homage to the shrine of Thomas à Becket. Some of the stories told in the office of the Menard House would more than rival Chaucer for broadness, but many of them had a point of telling quality right out of the soil of that country. The most humorous of them are scarcely printable. They were told by Engle and Lincoln. Herndon heard them and told them to my father.

The Menard House was within view of the shore of the Sangamon River. It stood all through my boyhood at Petersburg, with the barbershop of Hockey and Fricke next door to the north, and the law office of Breese Johnson, a native of Virginia who was creeping the streets when I was racing through them to school. One of his iterative remarks was that some newcomer at the bar "don't look like a lawyer, don't talk like a lawyer." He had that form of conceit, which lawyers sometimes have, that it is impossible for anyone to know the law but himself. I have often wondered how Breese Johnson ended his days.

The Menard House should have been preserved as a historic relic. But about 1920 the lot on which it stood was wanted for a garage. Hence it was wrecked, and sent to the scrap heap with the bones of Jacob Hofing, Breese Johnson, and William Engle:

All the old hotels are vanished from America,
All the frame hotels in a white-housed town.

The hotel on the corner with its awning all is vanished,
And the chairs beneath for loungers by the door on the
  walk,
And the office just a lowly room with worn-out linoleum,
And the barroom for smoking, and after work talk.
The eight-day clock with its dial dim and dingy,
The long writing desk with its green baize so fringy,
With the glassed-in advertisements

Of lawyers and of merchants,
And the register so spattered, and the pen caked with ink.
Gone, too, the fly-specked lithograph of Washington,
Gone with the chromo of the brewery at Milwaukee;
Gone with the opera house, supplanted by the talkie,
Gone the coal stove on its old piece of zinc,
And the night clerk old and clever, who seemed to sleep whenever
There were no late travelers who needed food and drink.

If there is a space where the voices of men and the sounds of earth are preserved, as upon a Victrola record, and possibly by some ingenuity to be reproduced, it is true—and this is akin to such a perpetuation—that rooms, old houses do not cease to exist even when they have materially vanished. If they can be kept in memory, why are they not still in existence? I think so of houses that are gone in Petersburg, and of some that are still there, while I am afar in space and time, such as the imposing Gault house on one of the hills, of Cap Gleason's crazy house, half frame and half log, which stood below the Brahm house, of the old cemetery, where Dr. Bennett was buried before I was born, of the Catholic church standing on the south hill looking down at the Sangamon, of the covered bridge over the Sangamon, pushed aside by a handsome concrete bridge. By the same necromancy Judge Hoagland, Henry Wilcox, the half-blind Henry Bennett, Breese Johnson, Jimmie Robbins, the lame cashier of the Brahm bank, and John Brahm still walk the square. Still the McHenry boys are having fights with knives and bricks. Still the dignified and patrician N. W. Branson can be seen at his window over Fisher's drugstore, as he studies the law. He was always reading in lawbooks, and there in the little town of Petersburg he became very prosperous, and his name went over the country for his learning and ability.

And T. W. McNeely moves briskly amid the scene, while Mose Nusbaum, who bought and sold cattle, is talking endlessly to the farmers about prices and prospective sales. Or here and there stalks Judge Hoagland, the county judge, always sedate and with something of a stare; or Captain Blane walks with military erectness here and there on his errands; or Cap Gleason, growing wilder and more incoherent, is being teased by cruel boys.

And then it is Saturday, and the rack about the square is crowded with horses and wagons and carriages, George Kirby's hitched to mules and Squire Masters's drawn, as always, by the white horses, Lena and Kate. Everyone knew their names. Business is noisy at Hainsfeather's Grocery, and the Broad-Gauge Store. Suddenly there is a fight, or it may be the day when Paul Bela, the saloonkeeper, shot Henry Katz in the foot to repay being cut to shreds about the face by a putty knife in the hands of Katz. Katz was a painter and paperhanger, sharing the patronage of Petersburg with Joe Pink. Yes, and I can smell the gas that came up through the iron grating in front of Homer Stewart's drugstore to remind an eager imagination of soda water foaming with pink cream, as well as to stir regret that the necessary nickel was not in pocket. Porky Jim Thomas may be somewhere in town, maybe at John Scott's saloon; and also Jack MacDonald of Oakford, who was noted for his skill in poker. If it be springtime a crowd of girls and boys may be going to the Fillmore Woods, in a valley at the edge of Petersburg that led to the Sangamon River, there to gather flowers, for there are flowers in great variety in Illinois. The pristine prairie was gorgeous with purple coneflower, orange lily, bluebell, the pink prairie rose; the last-named flower still abounds along the fences and roadsides.

In Spring when the blackbirds flock,
And cry along the rail fences, and in naked trees
The meadow grass grows green, and dandelions
Are sprinkled on the prairies, before the harsh burdock,
The cattails, horsetails, milkweed, mint, wild peas,
And pondweeds flourish; before the country lawns
Bloom with old-fashioned roses, and the lilac spears,
The ironweed, jimson weed are not awake.
But soon for miles white clover blossoms shake
To the passing breeze, and purple clovers scent
The April wind that hastens from the West,
Where flows the Sangamon. Then on the slope appears
Beneath great oaks, the spring beauty, by the tent
Of the May apple, and lady-slippers, which invest

The woodlands. But on the prairies where the roving bee
Gathers his honey, amid the boundless scene
Of gold and crimson and tender green
Blooms far and near the Wickapee.

On the rail fences bounding Bowman's Lane
Are bindweed, morning-glories, and yellow hosts
Of blossoms soon to fall, and turn to ghosts,
And fellow with the winds across the plain.

But of all blossoms of Illinois in the fields,
Or meadow ponds, or by the rivulet,
Under grassed hillocks, the wood violet,
By drifts of fallen leaves concealed,
Touches the heart most deeply with its hues,
Like a pale sky, its scent half unrevealed.
It is the state's flower, and it typifies
The pioneer who sought the river woods,
And struggled with harsh earth, unfriendly skies
For life and beauty in far solitudes,
And gave a lasting story to the Muse.

"Doggie" Dawson was a farmer living near the Masters farm. He was always in town on Saturdays. His nickname belied his obliging nature. For often when I wanted to go to the farm he took me in his farm wagon, which had no springs, and ran through the ruts and over the clods making the wagon bump. I want to know why I remember Doggie Dawson, who brings to mind the sunsets beyond the prairies, the strange thrill that I had as we turned out of the timber and saw the barn, the olfactory ecstasy that stirred in me when I got a whiff of apples in the old living room with its huge fireplace, the whole delight of being at the farm again? I could hardly wait to thank Doggie as I leaped out of the wagon and hurried to embrace my grandmother, who had been watching from the window and had come out of the kitchen to welcome me with a welcome that can't be described, and to speak to Doggie and thank him for bringing out her "boy." I suppose that there is scarcely a soul in Petersburg who remembers Doggie Dawson, and what can it matter, what can it matter if not one of us is remembered? A few of us get hung up in some memorial smokehouse, like my grandmother used to hang mullein, to be used later for medicine; some of us get put in rose jars, like rose petals, and for a time send forth the fragrance of summer days. That is all for this sphere of relative things. So it is with Doggie Dawson, in whose behalf I lift the cover of the jar and let people to whom he was all strange get a breath of his nature.

There were saloons all about the square, and in front of one could be seen on Saturday the little cart of McLane Watkins, hitched to its white horse. He would draw up in front of the saloon and yell so that he could be heard back on the hills, "bring me a beer, by God." Out would come the bartender with the beer. They said that he had taken calomel and eaten pickles when he was a boy, which had shriveled his legs. Anyway, he couldn't walk; he sat in the bottom of his cart on sheepskins, he sat at home in a rocking chair directing the work on his large farm and to very profitable results. It turned out that he always kept a pistol in the bottom of the cart; for one time a prankish boy threw a blacksnake into the cart, whereupon McLane got his pistol and fired as he poured forth terrible curses. He and his sister Sal fought in the courts about a crib of corn, which embittered McLane so much that he told her never to come near to him again; if she did he would shoot her. Sal could not bear to be dared, so one day she went to McLane's house, and just opened the door and thrust her foot in, saying "Yah, yah." McLane grabbed his always handy pistol and fired, clipping off her big toe. In town the men rebuked him. His answer, given in great spirit, was that his word was out and there was nothing else to do. "Think of shooting your own sister, Mac," they said. "Well, by God, what was there for a gentleman to do? I told her if she ever set foot in my house I'd shoot her, that's all there is to it, by God."

The old Greek fables have interpretations in Menard County, and especially the fable of Antaeus, the giant who could not be overcome unless his feet were taken from the earth. Hercules could not throw him until he lifted him into mid-air, where he was easily strangled. So it was with some of the rich farmers about Petersburg. There was one worth telling about. He inherited a thousand acres of land near the Masters farm, land that cropped as much as seventy-five bushels of corn to the acre. He tired of the farm and moved to Petersburg to run a hardware store. It took some years to drain him dry, and the people did not know that he was breaking and at last broke. Being ignorant of this, they sold him clothing and a trunk with which to make a trip to California. He departed, and never paid for these articles, as he never could pay for them. His feet were off the earth, with these tragic consequences. Let who will name other sons of Antaeus.

CHAPTER SIX

LET'S go to Sandridge, and see Oakford, where Porky Jim Thomas slumbers under weeds on a sand hill. In his day there was much drinking and fighting and storytelling at Oakford, and hunting of ducks on the Sangamon River about four miles north of the village. Ducks and geese abound here still. Here we are near the large farm of Ben Sutton, a great hunter. He had bottom lands full of pecans, paw-paws and persimmons in the autumn days. Hickory nuts and hazel nuts are plentiful anywhere in the woods of Sandridge. But pecans were then and are still a luxury. Here we shall be near Bobtown.

Sandridge is about six miles by six miles, mostly of beautiful prairie land, rimmed as usual with the blue of forestry. At one time there were three small bodies of water here: Blue Lake, Dodson's Slough and Concord Creek, which trickled along east through the Houghton and the Masters land, and went dry in the summer leaving crayfish to wither in the waterless mud. Blue Lake was drained and has been turned to cornfields, and that erased the last memory of Billy Paris and his wife Emily, and others of the neighborhood, who used to fish there for bluegills and the like.

The Sangamon along the north boundary of Sandridge twists and turns through heavy timber past Miller's Ford, Sheep Ford, Mussel Shell Ford, and the ferry once run by "Kay" Watkins. The remembered names of Sandridge are Pantier, Watkins, Armstrong, Hudspeth, Stith, Atterberry, Kincaid, Houghton, Kirby, Rutledge, Hatfield, Masters, McNamar. Magrady Rutledge, a cousin of Anne Rutledge, lived on a farm very near to Concord Church. Germans like Wiedeman, Deppe, Spille, and Boeker lived in the north part of Sandridge Precinct near the Sangamon River. Time and the wars have made little difference with these fertile fields, which still produce wheat and corn in abundance, while the meadows of clover and grass nod to the wind and the meadow lark soars in the light of the sinking sun.

But ah the landscape changes! Not merely by the disappearance of a barn or a house or a corncrib here and there, but by the vanishment of orchards, and strips of forest. Recently I was motoring in this country, and had to inquire how to go to the farmhouse of Sevigne Houghton. I had been over this neighborhood a thousand times, when I drove to Atterberry or Concord Church, or had walked to Hatfield's woods. But now the little grove by the Houghton house was no longer there, the old road had been fenced in, a new road had been made across the pasture which belonged to my grandfather. I looked about me and did not know where I was. And at the foot of a hill, where stood for years the tenant house in which Bill Schultz lived for so long, there was nothing but the tree which partly shaded that humble abode. The country had thus changed, like a face. To the north, where the Mason County Hills confine the Sangamon River, the osage hedges were no more, and in some places there were no fences at all. That country, billowing up and down, and once marked with houses and barns that I knew, was all strange. The Shipley Pond was dried where we fished, where the ducks and geese came in season, where once a swan sailed down out of the sky, and lived for a time amid the rushes of the muddy shore.

I'd like to know what it is that catches the imagination like a strange touch on the very heart, the very spiritual being of prenatal memories, that persist with reference to earth-places, like little streams bordered by willows, like fields of yellow wheat, like hills with the summoning sky above them against which may stand an old corncrib? Why should such common things stir down where there is no explanation in the heart? I identify them with pictures, or rather have the feeling about them of an illustration of Grimm's stories with all their power of magic to excite the youthful imagination. It may be the representation of a goosegirl in a green meadow, of a swineherd leading a pig, of a loitering boy whose hat has blown off, of a stream with willows beside it. There is in Sandridge a stream called the Lattimore, a nothing of a stream, which flows through the meadow grass, but in which there were fish when I was a boy. I placed the Lattimore on the prairie, not far west from the Masters farmhouse. I fished there once with Billy Paris and his wife Emily. We caught small crappies and mudcats, and then had our lunch, sitting in the deep grass. Well, I wanted to find the Lattimore, and I couldn't. It was gone, or else my memory misdirected me. I had kept only the Grimm illustration, where white clouds flew and the meadow lark and the killdeer soared through a magic sky.

Oakford is a village of a few houses, and a population of perhaps a hundred people, two or three miles from the Sangamon at the north. It was distinguished along the years by the fact that Porky Jim Thomas ran a saloon there, and by the residence there of John Armstrong, the son of Jack Armstrong, the wrestler of New Salem, and by the neighboring farms of the Watkinses, who raised race horses and observed a fine Kentucky hospitality. George K. Watkins, called "Kay," had two thousand acres of land along the Sangamon, and ran the ferry over the river. Many is the time when out horsebacking with my uncle Will Masters, the hunter, have we reined up at Kay Watkinses for noonday dinner, when we would be going farther in the afternoon to Ben Sutton's on the Sangamon. In recording Oakford, "Al" Cooper must not be forgotten. He was the son of "Widow" Cooper, and a wild youth he was. His animal spirits were too much for him. Evidently the pastoral monotony stirred the deviltry that was in him. For on occasion he would get on a freight car at Oakford, loose the brake and let it run from the siding to the main track, down to Atterberry three or four miles south. When the car attained a speed that made it dangerous for him to stay on it any longer he would get off and let the car crash into standing cars at Atterberry. Fortunately for him there never was a collision between the runaway car and an oncoming engine and train. But he was prosecuted for malicious mischief, once by my father when he was state's attorney. His fond mother went into her plentiful purse to extricate him from penal consequences. This Al Cooper finally made a name for himself in Petersburg, and the McHenrys decided to test his mettle. Knowlt McHenry filled his hands with bricks and waited for Al to come along by Mentor Graham's house. As he did so Knowlt began to toss bricks, as Al dodged and kept saying "Let up on it, Knowlt." Finally Knowlt ran out of bricks. Then Al crossed the street and disemboweled the enemy. Knowlt almost died. Only skillful surgery saved him. Al's case is better understood when it is remembered that in that day there was no auto, no movie, no diversion, except the occasional horse races, the church festivals, fish fries on the Sangamon, and the camp meetings. He had to do something with his superfluous energy, and that something was not driving the plow.

Jack Armstrong, the wrestler, must be mentioned in the annals of New Salem, but after he died in 1854, his widow Hannah with her two sons John and Duff lived in Sandridge. And there an intimacy sprang up between Hannah and my grandmother Masters, who always spoke of her as Aunt Hannah, and always with great affection. Later she lived in Mason County, and it was there that Duff committed homicide and was defended by Lincoln at Beardstown, a story too familiar to tell here. There is another story about Duff not so much known. It was told for years along the Sangamon. It was that Duff after his service in the Northern army became much given to drink, and when in his cups was wont, in order to get a drink, to show the discharge which

JOHN ARMSTRONG—FOR YEARS HE HAD ATTENDED THE DANCES, THE COUNTY FAIRS, THE CAMP MEETINGS, THE FESTIVALS

Lincoln had written for him at the instance of Aunt Hannah, who journeyed to Washington to get it. How Duff could have possession of a document like that, and how the archives of the War Department did not have it, passes all my guessing. The improbability of the tale does not detract from the delight of thinking of Duff at Porky Jim Thomas's saloon at Oakford showing his army discharge to get a drink. Neighborhoods, particularly those like Menard County, are full of charming fables. There are many about Anne Rutledge.

Hannah Armstrong moved to Iowa, where she died about 1890, and John continued to live in Sandridge, at Oakford, for many years, where he was engaged in the grain business. When he was fifteen and my father was about nineteen they became chums, and went to the dances about the country and over into Mason County across the Sangamon. For many years while my father was living at Lewistown he and John did not see much of each other; but when they were in the sixties and my father was living in Springfield they resumed their youthful intimacy, and went hunting ducks together along the Sangamon near Oakford, and in Arkansas for wild hogs and deer. They drove about the country in John's Ford car and up to Michigan, where my father had a farm. It was one of the most humorous cases of buddyship that I have ever known—these two old men talking and laughing, having meals together at John's little home in Oakford, where John played the fiddle in the most spirited and exciting way.

I had heard my grandmother talk about "dear Aunt Hannah," but not enough about John to make an impression on my memory. Hence when my father began to tell me about John, his stories and his fiddling, it was mostly new to me, and I wanted to see him. This never came about until one time when Dreiser was in Chicago, gathering material for one of his novels. I was then full of John's quaint remarks and stories, and when I repeated them to Dreiser he became anxious at once to go to Oakford. He wanted to see John, and down we went to the Sangamon River country. Arriving duly at Oakford, John was standing on the station platform. I had never seen him before, but I knew him by the pictures of him, and by his expectant face. He was glancing about with wild-bird eyes for someone that looked like his idea of me, for he had never seen me either. I went to him, followed by Dreiser, saying to him, "John, this is Mr. Dreiser, of New York." Dreiser turned his penetrating eyes upon John, who was not conscious of the scrutinizing stare, as he did not betray any curiosity in Dreiser, whose fur coat and New York apparel might well have caused a countryman to wonder. John was too much a man of the world, meeting all sorts of people along the years, to be flustered by anyone.

For himself, John was freshly shaved, he had on

clean linen and a good four-in-hand, his shoes were polished, and he looked eminently respectable. I might have supposed that he had dressed for us, but my father told me later that John was always careful of his appearance. Hannah, though a pioneer woman, had breeding, and according to my grandmother was a woman of excellent character. John had derived from his home environment under her an understanding of good habits of life, of a kind of homely charming etiquette, in particular of gracious hospitality. As a liver and a hunter, as a man who had gone about his own country for years meeting all sorts of men in that locality, and all the while proud of his father Jack and his mother Hannah, and of their days at New Salem, John would have been at ease with anyone. He took Dreiser for just another man, one perhaps of a new type, but no matter for that.

So we stood momentarily on the platform, where Dreiser's great height contrasted with John's low stature. Jack, the wrestler, stood about five feet six inches, and John was about the same height. John broke the silence at last by saying to Dreiser, "They say you're a writin' feller." And when Dreiser laughed and admitted that he was, John remarked, "Wal, by God, that was what I was told." John's profanity was continuous and emphatic. He went on, "Come on now, boys, we'll go to the house. Aunt Caroline has dinner about ready, and I've got some fine whisky for you. A feller give it to me over at the 'Burg.' "

We passed up a street where there were two stores on one side and some houses on the other. "You remember Oakford, don't you, Lee?" John asked me. When I said that I remembered perfectly, he went on, "Do you remember when Porky Jim Thomas run a sample room right thar?" John pointed to one of the stores which at the time was vacant. With this Dreiser exploded with laughter, to which John paid no attention. "Where is Porky Jim?" I inquired. "Wal, by God," replied John, "I don't know exactly where he is at. He died about ten years ago. We buried him here in Oakford. We'll go and look at his grave tomorrow." Though I knew why the man was called Porky Jim, I asked John for Dreiser's benefit where he got such a name. "Why, Cy Skaggs give him that name. You see, runnin' that sample room he got as big around as a barl, and as purple in the face as a gobbler. He drank a quart of whisky a day, by God, and said that no man could be healthy without it. Cy Skaggs called him that and it stuck."

Dreiser stopped to laugh, which John took as a matter of course. John went on telling about the last days of Porky Jim. "He had the dropsy, by God, the doctors called it, and almost bust. They had to tap him, and a man told me that they took off ten gallons of water. Once when we had a hoss race here he was here takin' bets and could hardly get around. The

Watkinses was raisin' quarter hosses then. 'Pears to me that is the last time I saw Porky before he got down at home."

John's house was only two blocks from the station. It was a cottage of one story, still standing in September of 1940. At the time of my visit there with Dreiser it was freshly painted and in good repair. The yard was surrounded by a picket fence. There were lilac bushes and other flowering growths on the lawn, and at one side was a vegetable garden where the stalks of last summer's corn stood, blasted and shaking in the February wind. Everything was in order. A brick walk led from the gate to the front door. From the chimney a cloud of soft-coal smoke was pouring. John opened the door, and we entered a small room with a low ceiling. On the wall were black crayons of relatives, of Duff and Hannah, of Aunt Caroline and of John himself; those portraits which stare so ludicrously, while protesting their importance and verisimilitude. Near the center of the room was a soft-coal base burner with windows of isinglass, through which the flames of a hot fire were flickering. On the floor was a rag carpet of many hues and in a good state. Everything was immaculate and in order. We could see into the dining room where the table was already set, and we could hear the steps of Aunt Caroline as she went about in the kitchen giving the finishing touches to the meal about to be served. John went into the kitchen, returning with the promised whisky, and almost at once Aunt Caroline entered, wiping her hands on her apron. She greeted me, by saying that she had known my grandfather and grandmother for years, and often saw them in their farmhouse, which was five miles or so from Oakford; and likewise that she had known my father, but not until now had she known me.

John spoke up, "This here, Caroline, is a writin' feller from New York. By God, I forgot your name." Dreiser told him in a quiet voice. "Yes," said John, "Dresser. Why, Caroline, you remember them Dressers that lived over thar by Salt Creek, just west of Dutchland. They was Dutch. Ain't you Dutch?" Dreiser admitted that he was of German blood.

Pretty soon the meal was served. I felt somehow that I was in the Rutledge Tavern at New Salem. John was re-creating the atmosphere of the past for me, and I was steering the talk so as to get that village and its people on the Sangamon into my imagination. We sat down to a table of fried chicken, boiled ham and boiled beef, to potatoes, cabbage, rutabagas, carrots and onions; to hot biscuits and corn bread, to wild honey and every variety of preserves and canned berries; to pickles made of tomatoes, watermelon rinds, cucumbers; to blackberry pie and many kinds of cake, to milk and rich cream, to coffee that was better than one usually finds in country households. John did not wait for us to begin. He started at once to feed, eating heartily, but not vulgarly, talking

JOHN ARMSTRONG TOLD OF THE DAYS WHEN HE CROSSED

HE SANGAMON TO MASON COUNTY TO ATTEND DANCES

without remission, and saying "by God" with the beginning or the end of every sentence. He told stories of the neighborhood, about the fights and the horse races, about his mother and her days at New Salem. I could not help but remark the manner through all this of Aunt Caroline. She did not utter a word, save to ask me or Dreiser if we would have more of some of the dishes. But Dreiser shook with laughter; he choked at times as John went on.

That evening we sat by the coal stove, where Aunt Caroline was knitting and John was telling tales of the country. Finally Dreiser asked John, "Did you know Lincoln?" John was born in 1849, after the New Salem days, and he truthfully answered, "Well, I kain't say that I knowed him. I seed him oncet that I remember well. You see when Duff was tried—thar's his picture on the wall—I was only nine years old. My mother, that's Aunt Hannah, as they called her, took me to Beardstown, whar they had Duff in jail. That's when I seed Linkern."

"What did he look like?" asked Dreiser, growing more interested. "Wal, by God, that's hard to answer. He looked like one of these cranes you see along the Sangamon River—tall, you know, and thin; and I have heard fellers say that when he was on the platform before he began to speak he looked dull like he didn't have no sense." "Did you see him sitting down as well as standing up?" asked Dreiser, growing analytical. John looked sharply at Dreiser, "You ain't no lawyer, are you, Dresser?" asked John. Dreiser answered that he was not a lawyer. "By God, you sound like it," remarked John sharply. "You sound like old Breese Johnson that used to be over at the Burg." "I wanted to know how Lincoln looked when he was sitting down, looked to you." "Wal, I expect he looked like one of these here grasshoppers with their jints stickin' up when they squat. He had awful long legs. Over at Havaner thar was a man named Colonel Prichard. He told me that he saw Linkern on the platform thar oncet, and that his knees stuck up halfway to his waist."

John went on without any hesitation telling about quarter horses, camp meetings, dances, fiddler contests, when the fiddlers did their best to win a set of harness, a whip, or a five-dollar gold piece; about the days when he crossed the Sangamon to Mason County with my father to attend dances there. The wind without was crooning, the darkness had descended by seven o'clock over the woods along the Sangamon, two or three miles away. He would have gone on talking if we had not asked him to play the fiddle for us. He made no excuses, he just got up and took his fiddle, and called to his daughter to play the organ for him, and give him the key. The daughter arose without a word, with no expression on her face, just arose like a wraith, and sat down at the organ and gave John the key. Then John tuned his fiddle, and sat back and began to preface the playing of each piece with some story concerning its origin, and where and how it got its name, and where he heard it first. For years he had attended the dances, the county fairs, the camp meetings, the festivals. These were the continuation of the New Salem events, and I felt that he was re-creating the past of the deserted village for me. I could imagine myself in the Rutledge Tavern, listening to John Armstrong tell stories of the Sangamon River, of Bowling Green, of Mentor Graham whom he knew, of William G. Greene, at the time not so many years gone from earth.

John played such pieces as "Rocky Road to Jordan," "Way up Tar Creek," "Foggy Mountain Top," "Hell Amongst the Yearlings," "Little Drops of Brandy," "The Wind that Shakes the Barley," "Good Mornin', Uncle Johnny, I've Fetched Your Wagon Home." He played a piece which he called "Toor-a Loor," and another which he called "Chaw Roast Beef." He played and sang "The Missouri Harmony":

> When in death I shall calm recline
> O bear my heart to my mistress dear.
> Tell her it lived on smiles and wine
> Of brightest hue while it lingered here.
>
> Bid her not shed one tear of sorrow
> To sully a heart so brilliant and light,
> But balmy drops of the red grape borrow
> To bathe the relict from morn till night.

He played the familiar tunes like "Turkey in the Straw" and "Zip Coon" and "Miss McCall's Reel," and he played a tune and sang words to it part of which were these:

> There was a woman in our town,
> In our town did dwell,
> She loved her husband dear-i-lee,
> But another man twicet as well.

John played a piece which he called "Pete McCue's Straw Stack," and he told us before playing it, "This here is called 'Pete McCue's Straw Stack,' named after old Peter McCue who lived down by Tar Creek. They had a dance thar one time and the boys tied their hosses close to a straw stack, and when they came out the hosses had et all the straw. They had been playing this piece that night, but after that they called it 'Pete McCue's Straw Stack.' I forget what they called it before this."

Resting at times from the fiddle, John held the instrument against his arm and talked, telling us what platform dancing was, and about the famous platform dancers he had known, one of whom, growing excited with drink and music, had looked about the room and called out, "Clar the cheers out, I'm goin' to take off my shoes and come down on her." He did so and his feet went through the puncheon floor and that resulted in renaming the dance music. After that it was called "Skinnin' Your Shins," for the dancer had skinned his shins pretty badly.

And John told about a noted strong man of

Oakford who had whipped a savage bulldog with his bare hands, and about Clay Bailey who had entered the circus ring at Petersburg and taken an escaped leopard by the tail and dragged it back to its cage. "He couldn't have done that withouten he was drunk. The likker made him powerful strong and keerless. Clay could whup ary man around Oakford. Joe his brother was a handy man too."

Aunt Caroline sat there knitting. She paid no attention to John, no more than if he had not been saying a word. The daughter kept her seat by the organ waiting for John's directions. Dreiser was red-faced from laughter. I was fancying myself back in New Salem when Jack Armstrong went about looking for wrestlers worthy of his arms.

John was as good a fiddler as I ever had heard. But he protested that he was a poor performer compared to his wife's brother, who had gone from Oakford years before. "As fur as that's concerned," John confessed, " 'Fiddler' Bill Watkins could beat me all holler, and he warnt a patchin' to my wife's brother. He used to play for all the dances along the Sangamon and up Tar Creek, Salt Creek, the Lattimore. 'Pears to me there warnt so much dancin' around Concord Creek. And fight! Why, by God, oncet over near the Lattimore, just this side of Dutchland, they was havin' a dance, and some fellers from Mason County had cum over to break it up. Fiddler Bill jest laid down his fiddle, stepped from the platform and whupped the whole lot. Now you see my pap, Jack Armstrong, was a powerful man in the arms, and the truth is Linkern never throwed him. It was a tie, and I don't give a damn what anyone says or any history book. It was a tie. My mother told me about it a hundred times before she died."

By this time I had looked at all the pictures on the wall with particular attention to that of Duff. It was a hard, wild face. Then John went into the almanac story, and Dreiser began to ask John critical questions about the almanac, where Lincoln got it, and how Lincoln got it in evidence without some proof preliminarily that it was correct. I am speaking now of the almanac and the position of the moon when Duff hit his victim with a neck yoke and killed him. There was nothing new to what John said, and in truth Dreiser showed plainly enough that he thought John did not know anything of moment. Moon or no moon, the question was: Did Duff hit his man? "You bet he did," was John's emphatic reply. "And I'll tell you why, by God. You see, this man and my brother was around here somewhere before that and Duff was asleep on a barl; and this man come up and cotched him while he was asleep, and pulled him off the barl. So they fit right then and thar. There was bad blood betwixt 'em. And that night when Duff used the neck yoke there was a general fight with several in it; and this here Metzger was hit with a slung shot by somebody, and Duff hit him with a neck yoke. But what Duff did didn't kill him. It was the slung shot. A doctor got on the witness stand and swore that it was the slung shot that cracked his skull. Besides all that, the evidence showed that Metzger ridin' home that night fell off his hoss several times. So how could you say that ary blow at the fight killed him? He might have cracked his head fallin' off his hoss; for as fur as that's concerned he rode home after bein' hit with the slung shot and the neck yoke. And Linkern's speech, which made my mother cry and everybody in the courtroom, freed Duff right thar."

"According to this the position of the moon had as much to do with the case as the astrology of the Babylonians," I said. "Is that so?" said John mildly, just as if I were asserting an obvious matter of fact. "Maybe you're right." Yes, Beveridge's thorough biography of Lincoln has the story pretty much as John told it to us. There were better things than talking to John about this murder case, and one was to have him play the fiddle. We asked for "Turkey in the Straw" again, and John played it with spirit. Then he played "Hell Amongst the Yearlings." "This here is called 'Hell Amongst the Yearlings.' I don't ricollect what it was furst called; but they had a dance over at Ben Sutton's oncet, and while they was a-dancin' the cattle broke into his corn. So ever since they have called it 'Hell Amongst the Yearlings.' " John furnished us with evidence of the manner in which tales and sayings grow up, and by that token how myths originate and flourish.

John, however, was not done with Duff. There was Duff's war record, there was Aunt Hannah's appeal to Lincoln to release Duff from the army, there was Duff's idle life after he returned from the war, when he fell into drink; and there was the matter of the discharge which Duff showed to curious loungers at bars to get drink. "Duff kept a-drinkin' " was John's comment. "He got so that anybody could whup him. He went around showin' his discharge from the army, and pickin' up money for drinks on it." John now laid his fiddle aside and brought forth some souvenirs, little things that belonged to his mother, a book containing Lincoln's autograph, a picture of his mother. It was the face of a dignified pioneer woman, not without a certain charm. That ended the evening. John was now tired, and it was his bedtime and beyond. So we retired.

The next morning there was a hearty breakfast served by Aunt Caroline, who went about and sat at the table without saying a word, while John laughed and talked interminably as before. We then went to the Oakford cemetery. I wanted to note the names of people I had known in the many long summers that I worked on the Masters farm for my grandfather. John then told me about a ride that my grandfather and George Kirby took from Sandridge to Tallula, all to see the family monument which

William G. Greene erected. According to John, George had come by the Masters house announcing that "Slicky Bill" had put up "the finest God-damn monument in the county," to which my grandfather said, "tut, tut," in his abhorrence of profanity. These two old men came at the last stretch to a road of heavy earth which had been rained on heavily and then cut up by wheels. It was as rough as a highway of logs, and the little carriage bumped and smashed the silk hat of my grandfather against the top of the carriage while George cursed and whipped the horses, "Get out of here, God damn you, get out of here." John thought this was enormously funny. But for the most part the fun lies in the characters of these two old men.

I paused before a stone on which was carved the name James Thomas. I remembered no James Thomas. "Who was James Thomas, John?" I asked as John came closer to me. "Why, by God, that's Porky Jim," said John, with a chuckle. So here at last was the man whom as a boy I had seen waddling about at Oakford with his near three hundred pounds of fat and his purple face—here he was in the silence of Oakford on an elevation of ground from which the woods about the Sangamon were plainly visible and all the surrounding country long tilled by the McDoels, the Watkinses and the Coopers.

I saw John again, and for the last time, some ten years after this visit. I was in Springfield on the occasion of my father's funeral, and John's daughter, who lived there, called on me and begged me to go to Oakford to see her father. It was very difficult for me to do this. The weather was cold, my time was brief, and I had for some reason to go by auto from Petersburg to Oakford, and the roads were bad. But John's daughter was insistent. She said that John was not well, that he was grieving for my father, and that I could solace him, and that it would be almost cruel in me to pass by and not see John. So I went, and owing to the train to Petersburg being late, and the auto making poor time from there to Oakford, on account of the roads, I arrived in Oakford at John's house as the sun was declining. John came to the door, and his manner was subdued; he showed that he was failing. I noticed that he said "by gosh" instead of "by God." He said "I kain't bear to have your pap dead. We knowed each other since we was boys, there won't be any more like him." He made a pathetic attempt to come to, he even played the fiddle when I urged him, but he was not the old John. It began to grow twilight, and I had to get back to Petersburg. He came to the door, saying that he was going to Texas the next week to see if he couldn't get better. I said to him that I was coming back in the spring and that I would see him. He said sadly, "I won't be here, Lee, I'm going to die. You won't see me no more." I took his hand and made fun of his forecast, then turned and departed as he stood at the open door. He died two months later, in January of 1926. Aunt Caroline lingered until 1935, when she died, and thus ended the Armstrong family, the remnants of the New Salem days.

CHAPTER SEVEN

LEAVING Oakford and riding south toward Atterberry, we are on our way to the Shickshack Hill and Chandlerville, all along the low valley of the Sangamon, a territory not very interesting or beautiful, save for the cultivated fields on the uplands. My grandfather built a little church at Atterberry. It is the village where I used to go with my uncle Will for tobacco, gun shells and fishing tackle, obtainable at Clary's store, which was still Clary's store four years ago when the Widow Clary was conducting it.

I may say that Shickshack was a friendly Indian who was buried in a hill by the river. He used to bless the corn for the whites by chants and incantations which dispelled corn-borers and brought the rain.

Between Atterberry and the Masters farm the country is as beautiful as any in Menard County, all with green fields in the spring, golden fields in harvest-time, with sweet smells of the clover blown from afar and from near by the long winds in the June days. So often I walked and raced the four miles from Atterberry to the Masters farmhouse, so eager to get there that I could scarcely contain myself. There was bindweed on the rail fences, horsetails, cattails and pondweeds in the pools of water. There was rich meadow grass, and in season dandelions, milkweed, ironweed, and the purple blossoms of the jimson weed. Around the rim of the landscape seemed to soar the forestry in that clear atmosphere. If I had taken time to loiter in the woods along the way I would have found May apples, wood violets, the flower of Illinois, spring beauties, jack-in-the-pulpit, wake-robin and lady-slippers. And just as often I have gone to Atterberry to take the train to Lewistown, grieving all the way that the summer was ending and that I was leaving my grandparents, my uncle Will, my riding horse, the carpenter shop, the pasture where I flew kites and scanned the Mason County Hills, or the house and barn of George Kirby nestled against the rim of forestry across the prairie. On such partings I sat at the car window watching my grandfather go to the rack for his horses. His hair was snow-white and had been so since he was thirty-five or so, and I could see this snow-white hair under the rim of his hat, as I remembered his voice, so tender, so deep as he bade me farewell. "Farewell, son," were his words. I was returning to Lewistown which I did not like, to school that did not interest me. And so my eyes dimmed as the train went on, as I glanced back to see the white horses of the Masters carriage turning the road to go on to the beloved lane of hedges that led to the gate and the door that had been mine in the months past.

George Kirby was one of the notable characters of Menard County. He was a man of sterling character who had gathered in about one thousand acres of rich land near the Sangamon. He had a good house, and near him lived sons, who were farming, and daughters, the wives of farmers. Some of his land was by Sheep Ford, and by the bend of the Sangamon as it touches Mason County. This land often overflowed in the spring and drowned his corn. One spring he planted corn three times and the rains descended and blotted all his work, then he cursed God.

Old Georgie Kirby who for forty years has lain
Beneath this sky, amid this boundless pasture,
    With rich blue grass for vesture,
His curses ended against the ruinous rain,

Which drowned his bottom land, and spoiled his corn,
Was brought to nothingness, as quiet
As the sky above, the fiat
Which made no answer to his blasphemous scorn.

Defying God he said, "In ancient days
You drowned the world, do it again, old devil,
And make these hollows level
With water to the hills, blot out the ways
And roads to town, throw open windows, doors
In your revengeful sky, and wreck my labor,
And flash your lightning's saber—
God damn it, I don't care now how it pours."

Georgie made for himself and family a burial plot in the middle of one of his meadows. Over what was to be his grave and that of his wife he erected a stone with the words carved, "At Peace." He went there to mow the vines, weeds and blackberry tangles one time and as he gazed at the words "At Peace" a hornet stung him on the hand. He howled with pain and cursed saying "At peace, like hell."

My grandfather and Georgie were neighbors and fast friends for over sixty years, dying at nearly the same time.

Six miles of sky divide the several graves
Of these two men, one grave is in the village,
  Georgie's is where the tillage
Still takes the flood, and where the winter raves,
And where the wind drives over the lonely plain.

Under six miles of sky you ponder
 Their God-mood, as you wander
Down hills, by woodlands and through Bowman's Lane.

In my autobiography, *Across Spoon River,* I have told about my father's removal from Petersburg to Lewistown in 1880, and what it meant to me in the way of changed circumstances and the loss of my chums in Petersburg, with whom I started in the old grammar school next the Baptist church, and near the square, near the old row of houses which must have dated from the very first days of Petersburg, where that branch of the Bennett family lived that followed the circus. Dr. Bennett had divorced a wife to marry the woman who became by him the mother of the circus performers. That was something that was talked about in my boyhood, always in a tone of censure. For one of the leading citizens of Petersburg was Theodore C. Bennett, the circuit clerk, who was supposed to regret the action of his father, Dr. Bennett. For the readers of this book I mention these autobiographical facts about leaving Petersburg for Lewistown.

But it happened that I did not lose my contact with Petersburg. For years I spent every summer on my grandfather's farm, plowing and raking, and hauling, and in happy association with my uncle, Wilbur D. Masters, with whom I hunted in the woods and fields, and fished and camped on the Sangamon. There was no one on Sandridge that I did not know, or know about, from Bowman's Lane to the Mason County Hills, from Blue Lake at the east to Oakford and the surrounding country to the west. Naturally the country possessed my imagination, and it does so to this day. It may be that I idealize it, but at any rate it has a magical appeal to me quite beyond my power to describe. I loved the people there then and I love their memory. In imagination I can hear their laughter, their salutations, the very accent of their words. I can see them as they used to gather at Concord Church, which was erected in 1840 by the Cumberland Presbyterians, who grew to be a numerous sect in Menard County. This church was situated about four miles northwest of Petersburg, and about three miles from my grandfather's farmhouse; and it was easily reached from Oakford and from Atterberry, which is almost in view across the three miles of level fields under the golden pour of the sun in summer. The silence and the pastoral beauty of the country there bring one into a trance. From the Masters house the road runs west, then south, then southeast, then south, then west, past the land of John McNamar, of New Salem fame, past the wonderful farm of Aaron Hatfield and David Pantier, whose grandfather came from Kentucky and was a fellow of Daniel Boone. His house stood back a distance from the road. Its broad outer chimney makes you think of old houses in the South. On the road going south toward Concord Church one passes the site of the house in which Andrew McNamar, the son of John, lived. He was the son-in-law of William Paris, who farmed forty acres of land near the place of George Kirby. Emily Paris, his wife, was one of those kind and utterly unselfish women that break the heart with recollection. One time my uncle and I on the way to the Sangamon River to fish were induced by William, who drew up at the end of the furrow as we passed, to stop for noonday dinner. He was willing to join us and have Emily join us if we would do so. Farming was of no moment to him; fishing and feasting were everything to him. So we stopped while Emily killed a chicken and made a gooseberry pie.

Andrew McNamar wrote for the Petersburg papers, sometimes indulging in humorous reflections amid his neighborhood news, that indicated a sort of Josh Billings talent. His brother Bill, the neighborhood idiot, was the most wonderful of all the idiots I have known. He was as close to the cosmos as the animals along the Sangamon, with that peculiar intimacy with nature that idiots often manifest. I shall touch upon Bill later when the present continuity is finished.

John McNamar, who figures in the story of Anne Rutledge as suitor and betrothed husband, bought eighty acres of land on Sandridge in 1831. He rented part of this to James Rutledge, Anne's father, and in a log house on this rented land Anne died in August of 1835. As a boy, when I used to pass

BILL MCNAMAR, THE IDIOT, WAS FREQUENTLY AT CONCORD

this site on the way to Concord Church, there was a brick house, now gone. In September, 1940, when I saw this spot there was a large sign in the yard saying that Anne Rutledge lived here and died here in the log house mentioned.

A little farther on going east is the site where John McNamar's house stood, even well along into my early manhood. It was a two-gabled affair with a sign on it saying "Salt for Sale." Often when driving with my grandfather I saw John McNamar standing at his gate, like a wolf looking from his hole. I do not mean by this simile that he was wolfish. I think he was just the contrary. Something happened to him in life, just as a tree can nourish a worm at the root. He was a successful merchant at New Salem; he left New Salem rather mysteriously for New York. He returned to Illinois about the time that Anne Rutledge died. If he had a genuine heart interest in her no one knows it. No one really knows his story. He was as shadowy as his face was to me when I saw him at his gate and my grandfather who esteemed him saluted him as "Uncle Johnny" as we passed. He would bring out stick candy to me when my grandfather relented and bought it for me. He died in 1879.

We go by a woods now, down a little hill and over Concord Creek, which empties at last into the Sangamon River; then up into view of Aaron Hatfield's great barn, a good man who was one of the heartbreaks of Sandridge and Petersburg. He had a farm mansion of considerable distinction just across the road from his barn, over which the swallows wheeled numerously year after year. He gave up farming in order to become a merchant in Petersburg trading 3,000 acres of Salt Creek land for a store. He didn't understand merchandising and lost money. Then he bought a gristmill in Petersburg, and there his arm was torn off in the wheels of the mill. He ended up walking about the square selling axle grease. He was reduced to poverty at last. His farm on Sandridge passed to some Danes named Grossball, who farmed with great industry and became well-off and prominent in Menard County. Aaron Hatfield shrank to just a name, and one in this day scarcely remembered. He was a son of Antaeus.

The Cumberland Presbyterians were the most numerous religious sect of the Sangamon River country in Menard County. The church was organized in Tennessee in 1810. Its influence and doctrines spread to the Sangamon country in the late 1820's, principally through John McCutcheon Berry, who was born in Virginia and served in the War of 1812. Gilbert Dodds and Thomas Campbell, both from Kentucky, preached the new faith along the Sangamon River. Dodds lived a few miles south of Petersburg. Soon the Sugar Creek Congregation was organized, and in time that of Fancy Prairie, Irish Grove, Rock Creek, Tallula, New Hope and Concord. For many years

Abram H. Goodpasture presided over the affairs of Concord. The church came into being in Kentucky and Tennessee as a protest against the cold formalism into which the Presbyterian Church had fallen. The revival party did not hear enough in church of the work of the spirit, and they could no longer accept the Westminster Confession touching predestination and infant damnation. Hence the secession. About a hundred years after the church was organized the Presbyterians convinced the Cumberland Presbyterians that they had abandoned their tenets of infant damnation and predestination, and induced them to return to the parent church. This brought to the Presbyterians the church buildings, colleges, money and property which the Cumberland Presbyterians had accumulated, including the church properties in Menard County.

The Cumberland church at Fancy Prairie was locked against the congregation, with the result that a suit in chancery was tried in which the Cumberlands contended that they had been tricked, that in fact the Presbyterians had not given over their Calvinism. The Cumberlands were defeated in the Supreme Court of Illinois. The court held that the courts had no power to interfere in the internal affairs of a voluntary organization. So the Fancy Prairie church remained closed, or was used by the Presbyterians. But I believe that Concord Church decayed and perished more by the gnawing tooth of time than by this litigation. As it was built it was a square structure perhaps forty by fifty feet, standing on an elevation above a little valley through which Concord Creek flowed. Around it and at its rear was a cemetery, called Concord Church cemetery, in which the Houghtons, the Clarys, the Berrys, Goodpastures and others of Sandridge were buried.

The Church had two entrances, one for women and children and one for men. Later these entrances were reduced to one, a cupola was added to the roof. It was modernized. Its old charm was taken away. Then it began to lean, and a large tree at the west grew through the wall and the roof. Rain poured into the room, the paper on the wall peeled off, the chandeliers were full of sticks and straw where the swallows had built their nests, the seats fell over or were twisted out of their places, the pulpit lay on the floor, having toppled or been pushed from the rostrum, hymnbooks and small Bibles lay scattered in the aisles, rents in the roof showed the blue of the sky or the stars by night. Concord Church became a ruin, standing in the silence of the prairie. I believe no malicious mischief attacked it, that only abandonment brought its doors to flapping in the wind, and gave over its cushions on the floor to the minks and the rabbits. It was not a place for tramps, for tramps could find no object in wandering in that neighborhood. It stood at last as solitary, as silent, as uncomplaining as the stones in the churchyard, with the solemn oak trees in front of it and the prairie to the west of it, with the Pantier house still standing; while the Pantiers and everyone who loved the church were gone. At last it was torn down, and now nothing is left but two concrete steps by which people entered the church, and a part of the walks that led to the steps.

As a boy, I often went to this church with my grandfather and grandmother. I entered with her and sat with the women of the congregation. My grandfather sat with the men, or more particularly he took a seat toward the front, for he was always called upon, especially on Communion Day to say a few words to the congregation, called upon by the Rev. Mr. Goodpasture, or whoever happened to be officiating. It was an affecting scene, that old man with hair as white as that figure in Revelation standing amid the seven golden candlesticks, with eyes as blue as a deep sky, with a voice of deep music speaking to that simple people of the blood that washes sins away, there standing so straight in his broadcloth suit and fine linen, while I shook with emotion to hear him and to see his tears, though having no belief in the scheme of salvation that his words expressed. But after all he did not assail his hearers with fear, he did not judge those who had not come into the church. He spoke rather of mourning men who could find consolation in the tenderness of Christ. There was no predestination, there was no ritual of salvation, there was no creed except to believe in Jesus as the Saviour. I have seen these pioneer men wipe their tear-stained cheeks as he talked. His utterance was a poem, and poems can always dispense with intellectual belief.

> Ah! Happy they whose hearts can break
> And peace of pardon win!
> How else may man make straight his plan
> And cleanse his soul from sin?
> How else but through a broken heart
> May Lord Christ enter in?

If there was a culture, a spiritual flowering and growth in the Sangamon River country it was among these Cumberland Presbyterians, these humble, generous souls, who in the days of Andrew Jackson followed him faithfully as their salvation from the evil plots of cities, from the schemes of selfish money-changers. They read the Psalms and the poetry of the Bible, and they sang the hymns of Watts and the Wesleys. Like primitive Christians they stood for moral virtue, good will, as the means of accomplishing what they regarded as the supreme object of life, the eternal salvation of the soul. Truthtelling, honest dealing, neighborly kindness were their religion. They knew little of the Bible, they knew nothing of history, of the blood rituals of pagan creeds, that among many peoples in ancient times the blood of animals was shed for the remission of sins. They did not know that in the sixth century B.C. Orphism believed in the sacrifice of Dionysus and the purification of man by his blood; that Mithra was a god in the ancient days before the Jews left the Fertile Crescent, who had baptisms and eucharists and twelve disciples. They did not know that among the Aztecs, before the Spaniards entered Mexico, and for centuries before that, there was the ceremony of eating the god, the sacramental bread.

No, these people and my grandfather grieved with a depth and a sincerity, scarcely to be described, that Jesus in his surpassing love gave his blood for the salvation of men. It was this grief of theirs that stirred me at the time, and even today I cannot think of them or of Concord Church without a surge at the heart. Their simplicity of mind and goodness of heart and implicit faith in the Bible seem to me a part of man's tragedy.

In the audience were the Berrys, the Potters, the Kirbys, and the Rutledges, who were numerous in the neighborhood, including Harvey Rutledge, whose brother John Will Rutledge lost his life while trying to save my uncle Henry Masters from drowning in the La Platte River near Fort Laramie, but who was drowned despite the heroic efforts. That was in 1862, a mystical time even in those days.

There was no organ in the church, the audience following some song leader. They sang "There Is a Fountain Filled with Blood" and a hymn entitled "I Will Arise" based on the parable of the Prodigal Son.

Through the courtesy of Mrs. D. B. Finney, and Miss Nell Carver of Petersburg, I am able to reproduce here the musical score.

These words give no idea of their moving quality when accompanied by the music, nor how they tugged at my heart in that long ago when those simple people raised their voices in a kind of pastoral sorrow as they sang them. "Buddy" Traylor, a descendant of the Sandridge Traylors, sings this hymn as he drives his taxi about Petersburg. But he has improved upon the words. Instead of "He will embrace me in His arms," he sings "He will take me in His arms"; and instead of the words "Oh, there are ten thousand charms," he sings, "Oh, I find ten thousand charms." Bill McNamar, the idiot, was frequently at Concord, and though he talked incoherently, he could sing with effect. The minor key of his voice lent a strange enchantment to his rendition of this hymn. He sat in the back of the church, decently dressed, keeping one eye always shut, his habitual pipe put away for the time. He always walked to church, refusing rides if they were offered him, just as he walked to Petersburg and all about the country, at any time of day or night. He belonged to the owls of Hatfield's Woods.

For the information of musical people, it may be mentioned that this song was composed by Joseph Hart, who was born in London in 1712. In his young manhood he was very religious, then he went astray, and published writings against Christianity and religion. The "apples of Sodom" sickened him and he could no longer drink "at the Dead Sea," as it is written of him. In 1767, during Passion Week, he had a vision of Christ in agony, like Lindsay heard Immanuel singing in mid-ocean when he was going to England. Under the stress of this vision his heart changed and he wrote this song, which is charged with penitence and heartbreak. A hundred years after his death in 1768, Concord Church was pouring out its earth-grief in the mourning tones.

"The souls of that people were their own Holy

Scriptures." Their theology was this song, it was "the poetry of Cowper and Watts."

I never shall forget the eyes of old grandmothers,
Who looked at me so tenderly
In their faded hats and cloaks;
Or Greenberry Atterberry whose voice with feeling trembled
When calling me a good lad, because he loved my folks.
I still can hear their voices as they sang of love excelling,
Of rocks and hills and valleys where milk and honey flowed,
And how beyond the Jordan was a fair eternal dwelling
Where the heart would find its happiness,
And the soul an abode.
This is the word as mystical as the coal borne by the Seraphims,
Some seed was from the Bible, but their hearts were the soil:
It was a flower of human love,
Of man love and woman love,
A separate religion made of hymns.

* * *

O Orphics, Orphics of the Illinois Prairies,
Of Goodpastures, Clarys!
O voice of Royal Potter, whose thundering tones
Overflowed the church as a goblet which brims,
In singing the hymns
In deep crescendoes and quavering whims!
O Royal Potter, O Royal Potter
What has become of your venerable skull,
Your resurrection bones,
Your judgment day bones and skull?

In the soft, dreamy air of September, 1940, it was a translation to another world afar from war, the noise of cities, the unintelligible movement of the stream of time, to stand by the former foundations of Concord Church and to hear the caw of crows as they flew over the prairies, and the crow of roosters somewhere by farmhouses afar. The rooster is not only the trumpet of the morn, he seems to be a herald that calls to the centuries, saying that many are past, that always new ones are approaching. All over the world, in Europe, in Asia, China, India and the Isles the rooster crows as the sun rises, and through the day. His voice sounds at Sandridge, at Concord Church, and somehow says that Bill McNamar walks no more, with his coat over his arm, his stub pipe in his mouth, his left eye shut, sometimes singing as he walked, speaking in a strange singsong when spoken to. When asked his age he replied, "I'm fifty, sixty, seventy, eighty, maybe. I don't know how old I am, I don't, I don't know." Then his voice went into a repetitious wail, ending in a sort of whisper and splutter. Often when riding with my grandfather we have seen Bill ahead of us swinging along, smoking his stub pipe. My grandfather as we caught up with Bill always asked him to ride. Invariably Bill would say, "I believe I'll walk, Uncle Squire, I believe I'll walk, I believe I will." And walk he did as we rode on leaving him in the dust that our wheels stirred.

My grandfather was his guardian for years,

AARON HATFIELD GAVE UP FARMING IN

ORDER TO BECOME A MERCHANT IN PETERSBURG

managing the forty acres that John McNamar had left to Bill. He lived in the house of two gables, lived alone. He wanted to marry at last and went to my grandfather to get his consent, which my grandfather naturally withheld. For years Bill wailed that he wanted to marry and that old Uncle Squire wouldn't let him "he wouldn't." At farm auctions, at the weighing of cattle, where men were gathered to attend to the stock, Bill was often present. The men asked him his age to get him to say that he was "fifty, sixty, seventy, maybe." They asked him about his attempt to get married, and what he did for a cold. To this he replied "I get some rhubarb root and bile it down, I do, I do."

And at last Bill had to be taken to the Poor Farm, where he lived till he was about ninety-four years of age, grieving all the time about his house and acres near Hatfield's Woods, near Concord Church. He escaped twice, but in his bewilderment could not get to the road that led from the Sangamon River to Concord. Once after an escape they found him asleep by a tree on the grounds of the poorhouse. He resisted being taken back to his room, where he lay in bed day after day—who knows? dreaming perhaps of the roads about Sandridge, of the Sundays when he sang "I Will Arise and Go to Jesus." One day the keeper passed the open door of his room, and seeing one of his legs sticking from the bed he thought that Bill had died. He listened and heard no heartbeat; he put his fingers on Bill's wrist just as Bill came to and exclaimed, "Take your hand off of thar." This was the son of John McNamar, for long years the wonder and amusement of Sandridge and of Petersburg, when he walked in for tobacco or groceries at Brahm's store. This was the son of John McNamar, who was going to marry Anne Rutledge, according to the tradition, though he went away from her to New York, and after he returned to Illinois showed no interest in her. It is possible that naturals like Bill have an understanding of nature and life so intimate and strange that they cannot express it. I can say that the look of Bill's eyes indicated that he was peering always into something that he had no words for.

When I was at the Concord Church site in September of 1940 I meant to pay my respects to the grave of Bill Schultz, who was buried there, and why I didn't I can't say. I walked about noting the names of farmers. It may be that not seeing his name—he probably has no stone—I forgot to search for his grave. But he lived for years after service in the Civil War in the Sangamon River country, and for a long time he was my grandfather's tenant farmer. He was pure nature, like an oak tree, patient and dutiful like a good horse. In my boyhood I spent many happy hours with him. His favorite expletive was "torment!" One time when I was helping to haul corn from a crib two miles from the Masters house we disturbed a nest of bumblebees, which proceeded to chase us and sting. Bill ran fighting them away from his bald head and yelling "torment!" I laughed till I could laugh no more.

About a mile south of Concord Church is the Old Concord Cemetery, where Anne Rutledge was buried. She was never buried in the Concord Church cemetery, though there have been chronicles enough in which it was reported that she had been. The Old Concord Cemetery is a small place in the middle of a field, perhaps a quarter of a mile from the highway. One has to cross a meadow of stubble to reach it, and climb over a wire fence to get into it. At once a large board sign confronts the eyes of the visitor, which announces that Anne Rutledge was buried in this spot.

Here for more than fifty years her dust reposed amid the silence of these meadows, under midnight skies when the owls hooted, when the field mice scampered over her grave. Winter came down and snow was blown through the swales, and piled against the rail fences. Spring came on and the grass grew green again, and the flowers put forth in the woodlands. Summer shone hot on the wheatfields and cornfields all around. Anne's cousin, Magrady Rutledge, spent a long life on his farm near this country cemetery and died in 1899, aged eighty-five; and Jasper Rutledge, his brother, lived a long life, part of the time in Petersburg, when he was a sheriff of Menard County. Emma Rutledge, the daughter of Magrady, was born, grew up and married Henry Houghton. He died, their children died or were scattered into the West. Harvey Rutledge, Magrady's son, married and moved away from the Concord neighborhood. All these Rutledges were familiars of my days on Sandridge. For years they worked at the plow, they drove about the country. The grave of Anne Rutledge remained. Not until 1890 did anyone pay any particular attention to it. Sometimes when I went to Concord with my grandparents, my grandmother took me to the Old Concord Cemetery to look at the grave of Anne Rutledge, which was marked by an irregular piece of stone with her name carved on it—just Anne Rutledge. But her story was mounting all over America.

Today it means more, perhaps, than that of any other American woman. Her humble life, her early death, the sorrow that was hers, as people imagined it, the enchanting romance of New Salem Village on the hill threw a surpassing charm and interest over her name. Lincoln's interest in her pales when the historical evidence is considered. But no matter, not Clodia, Beatrice, Eleanora, not Poe's Virginia, can match, at least in America, the fame of Anne Rutledge. It rivals that of Emily Dickinson. In 1890 the people of Menard County removed her dust to Oakland Cemetery, and put up a square block of granite at her grave. Henry B. Rankin, of Springfield, who originated in the Athens community, and for many years specialized in Lincoln memorabilia, had much to do with the erection of this stone. He wrote me for permission to chisel upon it the epitaph from *Spoon River Anthology,* entitled "Anne Rutledge." I was very glad to grant the request. Then he, or someone, changed the words of the poem, spoiling in one line the rhythm.

Standing in Concord churchyard one hears the crow of the rooster far and near over the prairie. Shakespeare happily calls the cock the trumpet of the morn, who wakes the god of day; but he is also the voice of long quiet afternoons, and in late midnights his lamentable half-wail and half-salutation seems to summon out of the earth and air the extravagant spirits of memory, and give an elfin and supernatural character to the landscape.

How faint, how far, how clear,
From Kirby's to the house of Oscar Spear,
From Houghton's woods to the dim Sangamon,
The rooster sounds his call;
To which a fellow throat
Sends up an answering note,
And another, and another, one by one,
Here, there so mystical:
Saying the night is passing, will soon be gone
Over the prairie, lit by watch-fire stars,
With all lights out in heaven's towers.

The wheeling night is gray gauze to the edge
Of the prairie, the hills, the river bridge.
The night is the patient moon
Down looking upon the meadow dumb,

Tranced with thought, with no words;
The night is the prairie's odeum,
It is the churchyard's rune.
The night is the peace of sleeping herds,
Near falling Concord Church, that stands
A ruin above the prairie lands.
These need a voice their secrets to express,
Their memory, sorrow and their loneliness.
The rooster crows afar, the misted scene
Cries out, unveils its grief,
And in a mood how bright, how brief
Dreams come of vanished hands
That no more bind the sheaf,
And centuries pass revealing what they mean.

And in the night at two, at three o'clock
The crowing cock
Calls, with no echoes, as even in a dream
Comes a long strain
Of music growing thin and yet more thin,
More far, more far away, more far away.
It hails the morn, but grieves for yesterday.
It is a voice half memory, half pain,
Like the summoning of the Gleam,
Like something lost, or alien, yet akin.

Those waked from slumber hear
That call far off and near
Over the prairie to the misty woods,
Along the river's solitudes.
They hear and turn,
Or out of the window gaze,
Looking if sunlight soon will burn
Above the horizon's haze.

Who-a-who, a-who—
It's day soon over the prairie land.
Soon will the cattle moo,
And the waking bird shake from his wings
The treetop dew
Before he sings.

In Old Concord Cemetery, near the spot where Anne Rutledge was buried, is the grave of John Clary, who gave his name to Clary's Grove, where the boys were tough and used to come to New Salem for drinks and provisions, in the days of Berry's store, and the store of the Trents. This stone is one of those extravagantly picturesque mementos that one finds here and there all over America. On it was carved the figure of a man in a plug hat, carrying a gun. He is gesturing with his left hand to a dog which is ahead of him and looking back; also there are words that John Clary died March 5, 1860. He was born in Tennessee in 1793. He came to Illinois and in 1819 settled by the grove which took his name, and reared a large family whose descendants still live in Menard County. On my last visit to Menard County I met one of his grandsons in a saloon; he told me about the stone with its carving by the grave of his ancestor in Old Concord Cemetery. After a residence at Clary's Grove for a considerable time John moved to Sandridge. In the meantime he was elected a judge of the County Commissioner's Court. Down to his old age he was a remarkable shot with a rifle. He was one of the best of the storytellers at New Salem. He loved companionable men and a drink on occasion.

From Old Concord Cemetery to Chandlerville on the Sangamon is an easy ride. In places there the river is beautiful, and not far away is Pleasant Plains where Peter Cartwright lived and died, and where he has a good stone to his grave on which are carved the words of the hymn by Charles Wesley:

> Servant of God, well done!
> Thy glorious warfare past;
> The battle's fought, the race is won,
> And thou art crowned at last.

He did have a warfare, but whether glorious or not is not necessary to discuss. He published his autobiography in 1857 through Carlton & Porter, 200 Mulberry Street, New York, in which he recorded that he was born in Amherst County, Virginia, in 1785, and that at first he was a wild fellow, a dancer, thought by some to be insane. In his sixteenth year he had a profound attack of melancholy which ended in his conversion to the Methodist Church. He arrived in Sangamon County in 1824, when Illinois was an unbroken wilderness, and Indians in hordes came to the Sangamon River bottoms to camp and hunt. In 1829 the Illinois Conference of the Methodist Church divided Illinois into two districts. The Sangamon District embraced Lebanon, Apple Creek, Atlas, Spoon River, Sangamon, Salt Creek, Peoria, Fox River Mission, Galena Mission. Cartwright was appointed to the Sangamon District, and thus began his peregrinations over Menard County and other near-by counties, which he kept up until his death in 1872, at eighty-seven years of age. He had a way of answering hecklers that infuriated them, and at times he would leave the pulpit to thrash an unruly fellow, then go back and finish his sermon. Once he was at Ellisville, on the Spoon River, where he had to flee a drunken crowd that pursued him. The river was up, which compelled him to take his carriage over by canoe and to swim his horse. He went on to Lewistown and there abode with Judge Phelps. Going on, he crossed the Illinois River near where it takes to itself the Spoon River; near Havana, in other words. Then he proceeded to Salt Creek, where the water was high. Again he ferried and swam his horse. Such was preaching the gospel in those primitive days.

Cartwright was a man of violent feelings and pronounced prejudices. He imbibed the fear and hate that brought on the war against Black Hawk, whom he called "the notorious Black Hawk" with no word against the whites who had taken Black Hawk's home away from him. Likewise he spoke of the "infamous deeds of the Mormons" and rejoiced that "an outraged people took the law into their own hands and killed Smith." A few words from Emerson on Brigham Young will correct this violence of denunciation.

In 1852 Cartwright decided to carry the gospel

to Boston, and so he went there. He preached at Church Street Church on the text: "Let us draw near with a true heart in full assurance of faith, having our hearts sprinkled from an evil conscience, and our bodies washed with pure water." These words are the 22nd verse of the tenth chapter of Paul's Epistle to the Hebrews. Later he preached in Boston at the North Russel Street Church, using the twenty-first verse of the twenty-second chapter of Job for a text: "Acquaint now thyself with him and be at peace, thereby good shall come unto thee."

It is clear enough from Cartwright's own words that Boston was not pleased with him. He was told in so many words by some of the "brethren" that he had fallen below the expectation of the audience. He replied, "I could give the people ideas, but I could not give them capacity to receive them." This was the retort of Browning when his poems were criticized. It shows that when a man is not understood, yet believes that he has a message, this is the natural and logical thing to say in Boston, England or Sandridge.

In his autobiography he reports that his course of training, where he learned theology, was in the wilderness where "we crossed creeks and large rivers without bridges, often swam them on horseback, or crossed on trees that had fallen over the streams, drove our horses over, and often waded out waist deep; and if by chance we got a dug-out, or canoe to cross ourselves, and swim our horses by it was quite a treat. O ye downy doctors and learned presidents and professors of the present day, remember the above course of training was the college in which we early Methodists graduated, and from which we took our diplomas."

Pleasant Plains is about ten miles from New Salem, and Cartwright was frequently there when it was a live village. He ran for the legislature against Lincoln in 1832, defeating him. Cartwright circulated the story that Lincoln was an infidel, and used Lincoln's devotion to Henry Clay to support the charge that Lincoln was an aristocrat. Later these two were opposed in the race for Congress, when Lincoln easily carried the day. That was in 1846. Notwithstanding all this association of names and careers there is not a word in Peter Cartwright's autobiography about Lincoln.

Cartwright made my grandfather's house a sort of station in his travels to the Spoon River country. He often took Sunday dinner there, and my grandmother had many anecdotes to tell about his quick temper, his racy stories and conversation. He preached his last sermon in Petersburg. My father heard him. The old man wept as he said from the pulpit that his days were ending, and even at an end. He died shortly after this. I do not rate Cartwright with Abram Goodpasture, as a weary messenger of peace, or with the people of Concord Church, where a form of sweetness and light really prevailed.

CHAPTER EIGHT

FROM Old Concord Cemetery we can go straight south to Tallula, where for many years resided William G. Greene, the most prominent man in Menard County to the day of his death in 1894.

He was born in Overton County, Tennessee, in 1812, and came to Menard County in 1821. He followed the Armstrongs and the Potters to Clary's Grove, which is near Tallula. He got back to New Salem and became a merchant. He went to the Black Hawk War, and for years was a student at Illinois College at

WILLIAM G. GREENE, THE MOST PROMINENT MAN IN MENARD COUNTY

Jacksonville, working his way and saving his money. When he left school he had enough money saved to buy 160 acres of land. He went back to Kentucky and became a tutor.

He founded Tallula, Greenview and Mason City. The New Salem days brought him into friendship with Richard Yates and Lincoln. He had been a Democrat in Kentucky, he turned to the new Republican party and supported his old friend Yates for the governorship. He became a railroad director, and collector of internal revenue during the War Between the States. New Salem, as it happened, was his good fortune, the source of all he became when used by his natural ability and energy. There he met the men who, as the wheel of fortune turned, became powerful and prominent. He accumulated great riches, and at one time was in partnership with John A. Brahm in the banking business at Petersburg. Along the way he had every comfort, and achieved every distinction that belonged to the rising rich at the turn of the century, a fine country place called Elm Grove, near Tallula, with acres on acres of prairie land stretching around his yard with its grove of trees. His daughter Kate went to Europe and saw Paris when that was an almost unbelievable thing to do. On account of his shrewdness he was nicknamed "Slicky Bill." There were rumors concerning his adept dealings with the Indians. As he and my grandfather were both born in Overton County, Tennessee, in the same year, they had these things as bonds of friendship. The distance between their houses took some hours to cover in the days of the horse and buggy, though they exchanged visits at times. Now half an hour will take one by auto from the Masters place on Sandridge to Elm Grove near Tallula.

Often when I was a boy I saw this product of New Salem. He loved race horses, and used to frequent the Menard County Fair, where he stood by the railing of the track making a mental book on the entries. His very black, piercing eyes, and his snow-white hair under a plug hat, like John Clary still wears on his stone in Old Concord Cemetery, made him conspicuous. It was only necessary to say "There's Slicky Bill" to appreciate at once the identification. Circumstances and mental disposition made the difference between my grandfather and Greene. My grandfather became only moderately well off. He hated all war and called all war unnecessary. Greene took up with the War Between the States. He deserted the democracy of Andrew Jackson. Greene was absorbed by the Hamiltonism that moved about New Salem unrecognized, for the most part, by the simple people who walked about its dirt streets, and lounged in its log stores. They did not know that New Salem and everything it stood for was in process of being devoured, and that Slicky Bill's career was a forecast of what would happen to the country at large.

Coming from the sunlit prairie, the bluff is reached that overlooks the Sangamon River which winds from the southeast, and then bends west striking the bluff. The bluff is of some height and gives a view of the hills to the east, and looks down upon the forestry along the river. It is one of the most beautiful prospects in Illinois, or anywhere in America.

No village in America rose as New Salem did, quickly and fully grown, nor vanished after a few years as it did, nor was restored and took its place as a historic shrine in America, as New Salem has in these last twenty years. The hill is covered with oak trees. Its top extends west into the level prairie. Ravines here and there cut through the hill, in which there are brooks like Green's Rocky Branch and Bales Branch. These flow east into the Sangamon River. On this hill, this ridge, John M. Camron and James Rutledge, the father of Anne, settled in the autumn of 1828. The next year they had the ridge surveyed, making some 49 lots, with a Main Street running east and west. What was called the New Survey, an addition to the first survey, contained 21 lots, with Main Street projected on an angle from the first Main Street. It was a time when gristmills were needed, and when steam power had not come along in that country.

Rutledge was from South Carolina and belonged

to the well-known Rutledges there. Camron was from Georgia. Both were millwrights. Looking for a place to erect a gristmill, they had first gone to Concord Creek, seven miles north, where Concord Church arose later. But finding that Concord Creek went spent in the summer they turned to the Sangamon River, which in addition to never-failing water had the advantage of being in a more populous neighborhood than there was on Sandridge. Clary's Grove was only a few miles southwest, Athens was about seven miles southeast, Indian Point about seven miles north and east, and Sugar Grove about ten miles northeast. For that matter Sandridge was only seven miles north. Petersburg was not yet in existence.

After selecting the site for their mill on the Sangamon River, Rutledge and Camron petitioned the legislature for the right to build a dam. The petition was granted, and then they built houses on the hill for their families and set to work to put together pens of logs, weighted with rock and sunk in the river, and filled with rock. What the geological story is of this part of Illinois may be condensed by saying that of the four ice sheets which reached Illinois, one hundred and fifty thousand, fifty thousand, and twenty-five thousand years ago, one of them pushed as far south as the Ozark Range. There is limestone along the banks of the Sangamon River, good for building. In the Paleozoic era was the Cambrian division, during which thick layers of sandstone and dolomite were deposited over the entire state. Some years ago I found in Rock Creek, near the New Salem Hill, a boulder weighing four thousand pounds and of composition so hard that it broke the chisels of the masons who smoothed its surface for the placing of a bronze plaque made by Josef Nicolosi, the sculptor, of New York. I had this boulder hauled to Oakland Cemetery and placed at the graves of my grandfather and grandmother.

There was plenty of stone and rock at hand for the building of the mill. Its pillars were made by filling log pens with rock, built up above the water. On these they rested the logs of the gristmill, which was set some distance into the river, not upon the shore, as the mill was which stood there when I was a boy in Petersburg. Next to the gristmill Rutledge and Camron erected a sawmill; from the sawmill to the shore they built a trestle of split logs. The burrs for the mill were made of stone quarried out of the hills near by. Thus the mill was fashioned.

And what a convenience it was to the people around! Before the day of the mill there was no way for them to get meal, except to use the pestle and mortar, or what was called a "gritter." That was a process that took much time and labor. But when the mill started to operate by the power of the Sangamon the settlers could have their corn ground by trading part of the meal as toll. And soon from Sandridge and the near-by neighborhoods, and from places fifty miles away, corn was brought to the New Salem Mill to be turned into meal.

There was a chance now for merchandising, for the selling of cloth and groceries, tobacco and whisky. And that John McNamar, whose story has already been touched upon and who was going by the name of John McNeil, and a man named Hill built a log store and started to sell tea, coffee, sugar, salt, blue calico, brown muslin, homemade jeans and gloves, straw hats, and dresses for women and simple millinery.

On Christmas Day, 1829, a post office was established with John McNamar as the first postmaster. It was re-established during the year 1940 as New Salem Post Office, receiving mail from airplanes where in that long ago Harvey Ross carried it by horseback from Springfield and on to Lewistown by the Spoon River.

Soon a man named Warburton opened a store, then William Greene embarked in merchandising and sold out to Berry. One of the Clarys, a brother of that John who was buried at Old Concord Cemetery, started a grocery store on Main Street, where he sold liquor for the most part. Soon there was a coopershop run by Henry Onstott. Then the Rutledge Tavern came along, and Philemon Morris's tanyard, and Joshua Miller's blacksmith shop. Peter Lukins, after whom Petersburg was named, started a shop for making and mending boots and shoes; Robert Johnson served the village as wheelwright and cabinet-maker. Martin Waddell made hats. Bowling Green was the justice of the peace, a huge Falstaffian man who lived in fact up the road north toward Petersburg. He made fun for the villagers. And there were the Herndon brothers, cousins of William Herndon, who ran a store. There were bricklayers and carpenters, while the medical profession was represented by Dr. Allen, and the ministry by Camron. New Salem at its best had about twenty-five buildings and one hundred inhabitants. It had the gristmill and the sawmill, it had a tannery and a quarry, it made shoes, hats and furniture, kegs and barrels, it spun wool. It had the Rutledge Tavern, and many boarding-houses, and several saloons. It had a cock-pit and a race track. It had Jack Kelso, the man who read Shakespeare and Burns, who fished the river and sold his catches, and went about day by day treating life as something unreal, and fellowing, according to tradition, with Lincoln, who arrived at New Salem in 1832.

It was April and a time of flood. The flatboat that Lincoln was steering down the river to the Illinois and thence to the Mississippi and to New Orleans got stuck on the dam at New Salem. The story has been too often told to be repeated here. It contains a symbol, as symbols are everywhere. Perhaps there is a Something that shows part of a whole, which the whole fulfills. The first revelation looks afterward like the first dim and small figure in a pattern, known by the Weaver and by the Weaver only, a figure that time develops to the full in the finished tapestry. Lincoln's life at first was as slow as the River, and it got lodged, only to be freed and sent on to the great sea of history. The people lifted his boat over the dam, the people lifted him to the presidency, the belief that he was of the blood of the New Salem people constitutes the sweetest part of his renown.

We can get an understanding of the spirit of New Salem by a description of its inhabitants. Bowling Green was born in North Carolina in 1787. John Clary, of the curious gravestone, married Green's half sister, and he followed them to Clary's Grove in 1819. He became a landowner, a justice of the peace in 1831. Mentor Graham, the schoolteacher, need not be amplified. There were the McHenrys from Tennessee. There was William F. Berry, the son of the Cumberland Presbyterian minister, John M. Berry, already chronicled in the relation of Concord. There was Samuel Hill the merchant who came from New Jersey, who was once the postmaster and the partner of John McNamar in one of the New Salem stores. He disliked Peter Cartwright, who was wont to sit on the steps of Hill's store and make unfriendly remarks about him, for Hill cultivated the drinkers. He fell out with Jack Armstrong and hired a bully to whip Jack, the pay being a set of china plates with blue stripes. Armstrong was a smaller man than the bully and finally was worsted but not until he had punished his man so that he wanted no more. When New Salem faded, Hill moved to Petersburg and there became an owner of the woolen mill.

Henry Onstott was a native of Kentucky and one of the few Whigs of the village. Thomas Watkins came from Kentucky, having been born there in 1789. He settled first in Clary's Grove, then in the woods near New Salem, where he raised race horses like Premium and Snow Storm and Paddy. His race tracks were at the edge of the prairie.

These people followed after Andrew Jackson. It was a time when America was devoted to the old warrior. In 1832 he carried Maine and New Hampshire, and New York, Pennsylvania and New Jersey, and Ohio, Indiana and Illinois; he lost Kentucky to Henry Clay, but carried Tennessee. In the electoral college he had 219 votes to Clay's 49. Delegations came to him in Washington, talking to him about what the people wanted. "The people!" he exclaimed. "The people, sir, are with me. I have undergone much peril for the liberties of this people, and Andrew Jackson yet lives to put his foot upon the head of the monster, and crush him to the dust. When I have put him down the other moneyed institutions will meet all the wants of the people. It is folly in the extreme to talk to me thus, sir. I would rather undergo the tortures of ten Spanish Inquisitions than that the deposits should be restored, or the monster rechartered."

So the United States Bank fell, and New Salem rejoiced, the mill by the river kept grinding, there was plenty of pork and hominy and whisky, there were wild turkeys on the river bottoms and squirrels in the trees, for good shots like John Clary to bring down. In 1835 the United States Treasury had over thirty-two million dollars on hand, and when the surplus was distributed Illinois received over four hundred thousand dollars as its share. It was not wonderful that the people were happy, that New Salem danced and sang and raced and hunted wolves on the prairie. They sat at the roaring fire of the Rutledge Tavern and heard the fiddlers and told stories.

I have mentioned Jack Armstrong in the relation of Sandridge. He needs a more extended notice in connection with the people of New Salem. He was born in Tennessee in 1804, and grew up to be a man of great physical power, though but five feet six inches tall and never weighing more than 160 pounds. He was lovable and sociable, like his son John of Oakford. His fondness for the tavern and happy company led him into intemperate habits; but it was his generous nature that prevented him from accumulating property. His wife's brother was one of the most famous fiddlers of all the country around, if not the most famous of all. There are men in Menard County to this day who will talk of Fiddler Jones, and of his performances at the platform dances and the country hoedowns. In the estimation of his fellow performers he surpassed Fiddler Bill Watkins. Elias Watkins, a fiddler living until 1941 near Petersburg paid his tribute to Fiddler Jones when I last saw him. Hannah, his wife, was thrifty and a good housekeeper, and a woman of great strength. When Jack was away playing or working she took the ax and chopped the stove wood. At times she lost her patience and scolded Jack, but she confessed that she could not stay angry with him. She told an old woman of Petersburg, long after Jack was dead, that he never ceased to be her lover, and that despite all his faults she loved the little finger of his hand more than the whole body of any other man she ever saw.

This is the woman who used to wash and mend the clothes of Lincoln. Harvey Ross in his *Personal Recollections of the Pioneers of Illinois* recorded that he met Lincoln for the first time at the home of Jack Armstrong, the wrestler, when he was carrying the mail through New Salem to the Spoon River country. Much has been written about the limited advantages of Lincoln. But what books could take the place of the friendship and association of people like the Armstrongs, the Clarys, the Rutledges? It was phenomenal, a miracle never to be repeated, that these homogeneous spirits gathered under the oak trees on New Salem Hill and built a village.

Perhaps the most interesting man of all the New

Salem people was Jack Kelso, whose wife kept a boardinghouse in the village. Jack was a kind of Thoreau. He knew the habits and the haunts of animals. He knew where fish could be caught in the river; he hunted deer and salted down venison. He knew the groves where the wild plums grew and the wild grapes, he could find the tree of the wild bee and get its honey. According to the story that has come down to this day, he read Burns and Shakespeare and introduced them to Lincoln. Caleb Carman, an old resident of Menard County, wrote ungrammatically to Herndon that "Kelso would often refer to that Great man Shakespeare allso Lord Byron as being great men and Burns and of Burns poems and Lord Nellson as being a Great Admarall and Naval Commander and Adams and Henry Clay Jackson. George Washington was the greatest of all of them and was his favorite."

What with the odd work that Kelso found at New Salem as a man who could do anything, he eked out a good living with hunting and fishing, and had a kind of simple plenty. He probably found happiness. His wife and the wife of Joshua Miller, the blacksmith, were sisters and the two families lived in a double log house which has been restored in replica at New Salem.

Jack Kelso had a lawsuit over the title to a hog, which was claimed by the Trent brothers. The case was tried before Justice Bowling Green, who decided it in favor of Kelso, saying that he knew of his own knowledge that the hog belonged to Jack. There is a story that some New Salem men got into a controversy about the title to a colt, and that Lincoln, who represented one of the claimants, asked Justice Green to conduct a trial "on view," which was to bring the mares forth and turn the colt loose, to see which mare the colt would go to. This was done and the colt was awarded to the owner of the mare which attracted the colt. Such was the jurisprudence of New Salem.

What became of Jack Kelso? He stayed at New Salem until most of its inhabitants had moved to Petersburg, sometimes taking a basket of fish to Petersburg. By this time the wild game was getting scarcer, the fish harder to catch. The country was becoming thickly settled. This was in the forties somewhere. He may have gone west. No one knows where he went. He disappeared with his brother-in-law, Joshua Miller, and nothing was ever heard of him again.

Go to New Salem Hill and stand under the oak trees and look at the river below and at the beautiful slopes of grass and grain across the river and into the tops of the great trees. The old dam is but a trace of stones, but the river twists and flows as it did when Jack Kelso fished in it. It still winds toward Petersburg by the hills, it still flows under the bridge, not the covered bridge when one could look through the cracks of the floor at the turbid and treacherous water below, but under the modern bridge of concrete. You may leave the river and see the Rhine, or stare at the face of the Sphinx on the sands near Cairo, or mingle in the crowds of distant cities, the Sangamon River still flows, it still takes to itself the waters of Salt Creek, and moves as silently as a blacksnake through the woods at Miller's Ford, Sheep Ford and Mussel Shell Ford, and by the place where Kay Watkins had his ferry, on and on to the Illinois river by which its waters are taken to the Mississippi, and thence to the Gulf. The New Salem Hill stands. No longer down it is there the dirt road which Jack Kelso used to get to the mill and to the river to fish; but now there is a paved road. Jack Kelso is gone. And because he went away, and became an uncomplaining memory, like the dead, there is still an emptiness on the Hill, something that begs for explanation. For the river flows on and Jack Kelso is gone long since into the silence.

There were the Trent brothers, who purchased the Lincoln and Berry store. Fred E. Trent, of Petersburg, wrote me a letter in which he intimated that the Trents were descended from a William Trent, a hunter and fur trader, who helped George Washington to build Fort Necessity. The New Salem Trents, relatives of Fred E. Trent, went to Petersburg when the exodus from New Salem took place. In 1841 one of them was an alley commissioner of Petersburg. One was in the army in the War Between the States, having before that paid fifty dollars for the Ferry rights at New Salem. They disappeared like dust before a storm.

When New Salem was restored, and made into the likeness of its old self, the planners of the enterprise converted a hollow to the west and south of the houses, the Rutledge Tavern, into a theater, using a natural amphitheater for that purpose. It is called Jack Kelso's Hollow. I was there one night when the moon soared over the oak trees, thinking of Keats and his words about "those green robed senators of mighty woods." The whippoorwills were calling as in the days when Jack Kelso lay on the grass and thought of the mind of Shakespeare, and what it made and could not make of this our life. On this occasion a pageant was given in which the coopershop of Onstott figured, and the blacksmith shop of Joshua Miller, as well as the schoolroom of Mentor Graham. Also there was a movie on the improvised stage—a movie at New Salem, which never heard of the now dated telegraph, or heard but rumors of cars drawn by steam. The oaks were "branch charmed by the earnest stars," and beyond to the east the Sangamon River was flowing. A night wind stirred the leaves. After all restored New Salem was like the body of Lenin in its glass coffin near the Kremlin. Its spirit was long since departed, the America of Andrew Jackson in which it thrived died, as America has died many times since, even since the turn of the century.

New Salem with its Tavern, its hearty people, its

wolf hunts and horse races, and wrestling matches, and talk at the grogshops, is Chaucerian material of the richest sort. There are other shrines in America: There is Jackson's Hermitage, and there is Washington's Mount Vernon on the shores of the beautiful Potomac. But New Salem Hill is a shrine to the pioneers, to the America that might have been, the America that Thomas Jefferson wanted it to be. To me the place is a heartbreak. As a whole, it is one of the most beautiful spots in Illinois, or in America. For one feature of the landscape is the broad prairie to the west, which stretches to the sunsets under a memorial light in which the Illinois meadow larks fly and hide and sing, breaking the silence of eternity which broods over the land with music that speaks of "old unhappy far off things and battles long ago," and of happy things as well, of hopes and love, of goodness and simple devotion to nature and truth.

Here on this Hill to blossom burst
A life all new, all pure American.
In western soil this seed of our loveliest flower,
Grown in Virginia first,
And on this Hill resown, produced the men
Made altogether of our original earth,
Being close to a soil whose power
Fed their diverging veins.
This Hill is loved, by history is revered
Because America sees its happiest strains
Of a people new, who briefly here appeared,
Simple and virile, joyous, brave and free,

Kindly, industrious, full of hardihood,
And happy in a sylvan democracy,
And purged of Old World blood.
This woodland flower cut down by drouth and frost
To cultivated blossoming was lost;
It faded with New Salem Town.
This Bethlehem of America, this shrine
Of a vision vanished, a people passed away,
Is loved because America here beholds
With adoration a freedom and a day
Which dawned and perished when it made the sign
Of what the land should be, and by what molds,
Its spirit needed fashioning.

What happened to New Salem? For one thing, Menard County was created and Petersburg became its county seat and began to grow. That was in 1839. For another, the Sangamon did not prove navigable. Boats like the *Talisman* and the *Utility* failed to make successful trips to the Illinois. New Salem could never be anything but a primitive village with no one but the farmer folk around for sustenance. The hunters, those first people to enter a new land, had come and were passing with the scarcity of deer and wild turkey, the first settlers, a mixed set of farmers and hunters, men like John Clary and Jack Kelso, began to move on as they heard the sound of hunting guns in the hands of strangers. They had, however, enlarged their little patch to a field, their first shanty to a log house, which had given place to the double cabin in which the loom and the spinning wheel were in-

RUTLEDGE AND CAMRON SELECTED THE

TE FOR THEIR MILL ON THE SANGAMON

stalled. Men like William Greene began to etch themselves out from the mass as men of influence and wealth. They were fairly educated, as Greene was, and the influx of doctors, lawyers and mechanics gave them a better setting. Speculation in land arose, and the land offices at Kaskaskia, Shawneetown and Edwardsville attracted the pushing and enterprising blood. Population increased rapidly. In 1830 Illinois had a population of 157,000; in 1840 its population was 476,000. Springfield became the capital of the state in 1837, and began to grow. Springfield, also practically on the Sangamon River, was about twenty miles from New Salem Hill. It had won the honor of being the capital of Illinois by vast corruption and logrolling, so that the era of capitalistic corruption was commencing. It had cost the state over six million dollars to move the capital. Like a great sea that beats with overwhelming waves on the shores of cities afar, great tides were mounting toward giantism and sending ripples of disturbance to New Salem. There was great speculation in real estate in Chicago and everywhere in the country, and there was great rage for banking and internal improvements. The Illinois and Michigan Canal was in the offing in 1829, and was actually begun in 1836. Railroads and canals were projected numerously and in all parts of America. The Illinois and Michigan Canal work brought hordes of Irish to Illinois. It took time to assimilate these foreign stocks with their race hatreds and religious bigotries. They did not understand the faiths of New Salem, they did not understand the institutions of the country. They spoke their own language, celebrated the feast days of their own saints, and took America as a place where liberty meant the right to do as they pleased. Antislavery agitation began to divide the people. Northern Illinois was filling up with New Englanders, who strove with the breed of New Salem for mastery, inspired by the fiercest hatred. Trouble about Texas was brewing. Speculation and banks had sapped the country, and a panic was impending, which descended upon the land in 1837. In 1836 Van Buren had won 170 electoral votes for the presidency, against 73 given to Harrison the soldier, to 26 given to Hugh L. White the Whig candidate, who was supported by Lincoln. New Salem remained loyal to Andrew Jackson. The Whig party, organized on the dishonest pretense that Jackson was a tyrant and that they sought to preserve America from Toryism, as the English Whigs had done in the days of Charles II, produced the smallest men that America has seen in politics. When Harrison was elected the Washington *Globe* lamented, "for the first time in the history of the Republic the power of money has triumphed over intelligence. Democracy has been beaten by a new description of voters, some of flesh and blood and bones and others of mere straw. The former raked and scraped from the jails and penitentiaries had been gathered at log cabin rendezvous and organized for action. The latter were the pipe-layers, the illegal voters, the fraudulent voters trained to perpetuate fraud by voting twice, changing their names and dress, going to different polls, putting in two votes and using every device the ingenuity of man could devise. The Bourbons are restored. For the first time since the adoption of the Constitution a Democratic President has been defeated when placed before the people. . . . No more may the world see coons, cabins, and cider usurp the place of principles, nor doggerel verse elicit a shout while reason is passed with a sneer! Had we been beaten in a fair field by such men as Webster or Clay, by manly argument, we should feel but half the mortification we do at being beaten by such a man as Harrison."

Whiggery, having emerged in 1834, was triumphant in 1840. The fake log cabin had won the day. They had stolen the coonskin cap, the fiddlers by the fireplace of New Salem, and in that masquerade they had marched to the mastery of America. Andrew Jackson principles after a long period of success were relegated. In 1830 there were only four anti-Jackson legislatures in the country, namely in Vermont, Massachusetts, Connecticut and Delaware. In the six years from 1830 to 1836 twenty-seven states held 162 sessions of their legislatures. Of these 118 had Jackson majorities, 40 anti-Jackson, and 4 Calhoun. The people of this period were happy and prosperous, as

New Salem was. They had no heavy cares, no political anxieties. They cared nothing about other countries, about China, Japan, about England or Germany, about Europe. In 1834 the prosperity of the country was immense. John Quincy Adams said, "The prosperity of the country, independent of all agency of the government, is so great that the people have nothing to disturb them but their own waywardness and corruption."

All of this happy state of men was blown away by lies, and New Salem's decline may be considered as a feature of the change, even if these lies did nothing directly to the village on the hill. A direct cause of the fall of New Salem was the incorporation of Petersburg, which quickly began to grow. It had a place on the river as advantageous, and in some respects as beautiful, as that of New Salem. It soon became the county seat of Menard, and as it was but two miles away from New Salem there was no need of two post officers so near together. The New Salem post office was removed to Petersburg in 1836. It never could have paid, for in the year 1833 the receipts of the Chicago office were only $369, and those of Beardstown and Peoria $187 and $136, respectively. The receipts of the New Salem post office must have been less.

Besides what has been detailed, there must have been other reasons for the abandonment of New Salem, seeing that little hamlets like Atterberry and

Oakford on the prairie have continued to live. Things can be told in special, like the removal of the Rutledges to Concord, like the death of Bowling Green in 1841, like the vanishment of the Armstrongs to Sandridge. All these things are concrete, but something remains, as if the Muse of History touched the village with her hand, bringing it to sleep, and charming the log houses to fall, and the grass to grow again in front of the Rutledge Tavern. For the end of New Salem came with a suddenness, after the end had been prepared by removals to Petersburg, comparable to the disappearance of Jack Kelso. There is nothing more silent in the world than the sunlit air over the restored village, nothing more symbolical of endless time than the continuous flow of the Sangamon below the Hill, the very river in which Jack Kelso fished and by which John Clary hunted in the days of wolves and deer.

When I was a boy in Petersburg only the ruins of the Rutledge Tavern remained. We saw its leaning walls, we boys as we tramped the pasture that surrounded it, and lay in dreams under the summer sun. Rotting logs here and there had fallen from the walls of the decayed log houses of Dr. Allen, William Berry, Peter Lukins, the Herndon brothers, John McNamar and the others. Here and there were remnants of the limestone foundations, sticking above a growth of weeds. All this meant little or nothing to us. What we were fascinated by was the mill whose wheels were turned by the Sangamon. There we could hear the burrs go round, there we could see the meal and flour pour forth, there we could hear the rushing of the water under the mill, which turned the wheels. This was the mill constructed in 1852.

So New Salem decayed and slept, and Petersburg grew and prospered. By 1840 only ten buildings of the village remained; by 1845 only the Rutledge Tavern was standing, which was probably the first structure to be erected on the Hill. The Petersburg Committee on Sites found the foundations of the Berry store, the building itself having been moved to Petersburg long before and set up back of Bishop's Gunshop on the south side of the square. They found the foundations of Offut's store, and the location of the cockpit, which was midway between the Offut and the Clary store. They found where the gander-pulling contests were conducted. It was south of the Offut store. They identified the horse-racing course on Main Street, from which it ran into the travel road north and south down the Hill north to the Spoon River, Havana and Lewistown, and south to Springfield. Surveyors were called in to locate the sites of houses, for the real estate records showed the transfers of lots, and the original survey of New Salem was also on the public records.

In 1906, William Randolph Hearst came to the Old Salem Chautauqua to deliver a lecture. The Old Salem Chautauqua grounds were on the other side of the river from New Salem Hill. There the river bends on its way toward Athens, and nearer Petersburg. Mr. Hearst saw the advantage of preserving the New Salem site. So he purchased the sixty acres which constituted it and gave it to the Old Salem Chautauqua Association. When the Old Salem Lincoln League was chartered in 1918, Mr. Hearst consented to the transfer of the village site to the state of Illinois, to be made into a public park, all this free and in trust for the public. The restoration of the village followed. Even the old well in front of the Rutledge Tavern was found, cleaned out and reclaimed. The Berry and other stores were given shelves and counters, and barrels for flour and sugar, and counter scales for weighing. The country was scoured for authentic spinning wheels and old looms. In the museum building was placed a side-saddle, said to be the one which Anne Rutledge used. Chairs, tables, bedsteads, clocks of the thriving period of New Salem were gathered up, as well as boot-jacks, potato mashers, butter bowls; churns and candle molds were added to make real the setting of the old homes, the stores and the inn. The rail fence, sometimes called the rail and rider fence, was built around garden spots, just as they existed on Sandridge and other parts of Menard County before hedges and barbed wire were used for enclosing fields. There is a rail fence near the Rutledge Tavern, and as it laces the sky and stands against the surrounding scene, the primitive conditions are conjured in the sudden magic of a glimpse.

Thus today New Salem is as nearly like it was in the 1830's as it can be made by money, devoted care and intelligent research into the past. Known as New Salem Park, it attracts thousands of tourists every year, particularly in the good weather of the seasons. Hundreds of people wander daily through the streets, and enter the log cabins and the stores to see what the village was in the long ago. There is nothing more beautiful in America, and nothing so unique. It is a shrine to pioneer America.

It was between 1820 and 1830 that settlement spread northward in Illinois from the southern states to the Sangamon River region. In 1823, Springfield was only a frontier village of a dozen log cabins, Peoria had but a few families, and Chicago was a military and trading post. The rest of northern Illinois was mostly unoccupied. Then in the late twenties came the influx of people into the Sangamon country attracted by the fertility of the land. By 1837, Springfield had 1,500 people. As the prairies fascinated William Cullen Bryant, so they aroused the wonder of the pioneers. And yet the prairie presented difficulties. Timber was needed for building, running water for stock or mills; the prairie afforded no protection in winter against the bitter winds and driving snow. With the growth of population the woods became filled, and the day of the hunter was fading. Newcomers by necessity crowded out upon the prairies, which soon encircled the woodland with a belt of farms. Soon ring after ring of farms was established inside the first, and farther into the prairie, until the whole prairie was occupied. My grandmother told me that when she arrived on Sandridge and looked over the lonely stretch of billowing land north to the Mason County Hills along the Sangamon River her heart sank. But when miles of corn began to wave their banners, and the land was diversified by houses and barns and divided by rail fences, the scene became beautiful, the country became prosperous.

These things considered it can be seen what the advantages were of New Salem village: it was in the woods, it was near the prairie, it was on a river. One of the greatest problems that the pioneer faced was the matter of transportation of his produce to a market. All of this country is in the Illinois River valley, and that river was the only connection between it and the outside world. Hence the early settlements were made near the rivers. The steamboat was on its way. The Erie Canal was a going concern in 1825. By 1834 floods of settlers from the East began to arrive by boat at the village of Chicago. The Sangamon River felt all this. The navigability of the river became a pressing subject of discussion. For Springfield and New Salem were a considerable distance from the Illinois River. It was about 90 miles by the Sangamon from Petersburg to the Illinois. The roads were very poor, deep with mud in the fall, winter and spring, and heavy with dust in the summer. In that time the rainfall was heavier than it was later, and the Sangamon in consequence was deeper and fuller. Navigation of the river seemed feasible.

On February 19, 1832, there was an announcement in the Cincinnati *Gazette* in these words: "The splendid upper cabin steamer *Talisman*, J. M. Pollock master, will leave for Portland, Springfield on the Sangamon River, and all intermediate points and landings, say Beardstown, Naples, St. Louis, Louisville, on Thursday, February 2. For freight or passage apply to Captain Vincent A. Bogue at the Broadway Hotel or to Allison Owen."

On March 29, 1832, the Springfield *Journal* said: "On Saturday last the citizens of this place [Springfield] were gratified by the arrival of the steamer *Talisman*, J. W. Pollock, master, of 150 tons burden, at the Portland landing opposite this town. The safe arrival of a boat of the size of the *Talisman* on a river never before navigated by steam had created much solicitude, and the shores for miles were crowded by our citizens. Her arrival at the destined port was hailed with loud acclaim and full demonstrations of pleasure. When Captain Bogue located his steam mill on the Sangamon River twelve months ago, and asserted his determination to land a steamboat there within a year, the idea was considered chimerical by some, and utterly impracticable by others."

A writer of verse at Springfield made the vaunt:

And I will make our Sangamo
Outshine in verse the famous Po.

However, in going to Springfield the *Talisman* stuck on the dam at New Salem. A part of the cargo was removed, and by means of a cable and a capstan the boat was pulled off, and proceeded without any more trouble to Cotton Hill just east of Springfield. Then the *Talisman* returned to the Illinois River. The Sangamon had been navigated, but nothing came of it after all. In April, 1832, the *Talisman* was burned at Alton.

In 1836, five years after the journey of the *Talisman,* the steamer *Utility* came up the Sangamon as far as Petersburg. The water was low and the progress of the boat difficult. The captain was afraid to start back for the Illinois. He sold the *Utility* to John Taylor, a citizen of Petersburg, who used it to build the first house that was built in Petersburg. The first glass windows of the town came out of this boat, and the first steam mill in the town, or in Menard County, was run by the engine of the abandoned *Utility.*

By 1836 railroads were coming into Illinois. In that year the Galena and Chicago Union Railroad was chartered. In the same year the Illinois Central was chartered, but collapsed and remained moribund until 1850. William G. Greene, of Tallula, was made president of the Petersburg and Tonica Railroad, organized in 1856; and later was an officer of the Springfield and Northwestern, organized in 1852, a road that ran from Havana through Oakford, Atterberry and Petersburg by the shore of the Sangamon River between Petersburg and Athens. Notwithstanding all this, the navigation of the Sangamon was agitated in 1853. In that year a subscription of $5,000 was taken up in Petersburg to make the Sangamon navigable. In April a boat called *The Wave* arrived at Petersburg, and it was said that it had no difficulty for want of water in the river, which was four feet deep, but that obstructions from drifts and narrow turns presented obstacles. These could be readily obviated.

Steamboating in its real glory lasted only thirty years on the Mississippi, and then the railroad spelled its doom. How could the little Sangamon hope to send boats up and down from Springfield to Alton—how against the changes that took the life of New Salem village?

The first schoolhouse in the territory which became Menard County was built at Sugar Grove, in which the village of Fancy Prairie was located. The schoolhouse of New Salem was near the village, but not in it. All the schoolhouses of the period were made of split logs, covered with boards held in place by weight poles; the floor was of puncheons, made of split logs, the seats were made of the half of a log, ten or twelve feet long, with four pins set for legs in auger holes. The writing desk was a slab set on two large pins laid in a slanting position. The books used were the New Testament, Pike or Smiley's Arithmetic, Webster's Old Speller, and Murray or Kirkham's Grammar. At a very early time the North Sangamon Academy was founded at Indian Point, seven or eight miles from New Salem. This was the work of the Presbyterian Church. My father studied geometry and Vergil there before he went to Ann Arbor in the sixties. The buildings of this academy, one a substantial brick structure two stories high, were in existence a few years ago, standing in a beautiful grove of oak trees, on the edge of Indian Creek.

But as for educational facilities, New Salem had Illinois College at Jacksonville, thirty miles or so away, which was organized in 1829 by some Yale graduates. The first president was the Reverend Edward Beecher, the brother of Henry Ward Beecher. David Rutledge, Anne's brother, was a student there. There was also at Jacksonville the Jacksonville Female Academy founded in 1835, and Knox Manual Labor College (1837) at Galesburg in the Spoon River country.

CHAPTER NINE

THE HOUSES along the Sangamon River were at first the "three-faced" camps; then came the log houses. The cracks were filled with pieces of wood called chinks, and then daubed over with mortar made of clay. Sometimes the floor was nothing more than hard-tramped earth. I saw many such log cabins in and around Sandridge. Sometimes the floor was made of puncheons, which were split logs with the split side turned up. The roof was laid with clapboards, held down by weight poles. The fireplace was

THE LONG EVENINGS AT NEW SALEM WERE BROKEN

N THEIR QUIET BY THE BAT-BAT OF WOODEN LOOMS

contrived by cutting a space in the wall of the room, a space of five or six feet, three sides of which were built up by logs, making an offset in the wall. This was lined with dirt, or stone. The flue was built of small sticks plastered over with mud. The door was an opening made by cutting out the logs in one side of the room. The hinges were of wood, while the fastening consisted of a wooden latch. To enable the occupants to open the door from the outside, a buckskin string was tied to the latch bar and passed through a small hole above it, so that when the string was pulled from the outside it lifted the latch out of the hook, and the door opened. At night when it was desirable to lock the door the string was drawn through the hole and all was considered safe.

George Spears, of Clary's Grove, built a brick house in 1829. It was the first brick house in Menard County. Mud for the bricks was tramped by oxen. The lumber was sawed by hand by a whipsaw. All the flooring of blue ash and all the finishing lumber of walnut, and the sheeting for the roof were produced by the whipsaw. This house was built so substantially that fifty years after its erection it looked new. Spears sent to St. Louis for glass for the windows. Glass at the time was little known. The log houses pasted greased paper over an unclosed crack in the wall.

In the restored houses of New Salem one may see the flat oven, the frying pan, the iron pot, the coffee pot, which constituted the cooking equipment of a New Salem kitchen. The oven was set on a bed of coals. The housewife took stiff Indian dough in her hands, deftly patting it from hand to hand into the required shape. Then she tossed it into the oven, and it came out "dodgers." As soon as the bread was done it was taken out on a tin platter and set by the coals of the fire to keep it warm. The venison or ham, the squirrel or duck, was then cooked in the oven. In the grease that remained in the oven from the meats, lye hominy was cooked—lye hominy made by soaking Indian corn in the lye of wood ashes until the outer hulls peeled off, leaving a pure white kernel. Sugar was unknown, but wild honey was plentiful, in some sections, but at New Salem there was maple sugar. The bees were thick around the New Salem Hill, and wherever there was timber. Wild crabs, wild grapes and various kinds of berries were often preserved in honey. For years wheat bread was unknown. But the hunters and storekeepers of New Salem lived fat. Jack Kelso's wife is said to have been a famous cook, and the same thing has come down to us concerning Hannah Armstrong.

The stores of New Salem dealt in various kinds of cloth, calico and the like. But at an early day and up to the time of New Salem men wore trousers and shirts of buckskin, and caps of coon- or foxskin. Both men and women wore moccasins. At first cotton goods were hard to get. They had to be brought from a distance. The soil of Menard County was not adapted to cotton. But flax could be raised, and it was raised. The women spun this flax into good linen, which was made into underwear, towels and cloth. There were also vast fields of wild nettle, which made an excellent lint, that could be easily bleached and woven. Thousands of yards of linen were made from these nettles over the breadth of Menard County. One housewife of Sugar Grove spun thirty yards of this linen. With flax raised in a sufficient quantity and with the increase in sheep, Menard County had enough material for cloth. The problem then was to spin it and weave the cloth. Trousers and jackets made of deerskin had disadvantages. If they got wet and then were dried out they shrank and were hard, and rattled as the wearer walked. After the deerskin apparel came blue jeans, colored with the bark of young shoots of the walnut, whence came the word "butternut" as applied to this material, which was worn so extensively then.

Every family, nearly, had its own spinning wheel, with winding blades, reel, warping bars made by driving pins into the wall, and wooden looms. The long evenings at New Salem were broken in their quiet by the whir of the wheels, by the bat-bat of the loom.

The moon and stars are shining on the Hill, or the clouds are drifting over it. But the rooms of the log houses are full of charm and happiness. If the weather be cold a bright fire burns on the wide hearth, and the great flames leap up the wooden chimney making light enough for the work of the head of the house, who is making shoes, or for the daughter, who is drawing out the long woolen threads from the wheel which is filling the room with its musical drone. There may be a fiddler by the fire, who during the day has been hunting on the bottoms, but now after the evening meal is playing "Buffalo Gals," "The Irish Wash Woman," "Sugar in the Gourd," "The Devil's Dream," "Nigger in the Woodpile," "Miss McCall's Reel," as along the years those tunes were played by Harry Taylor of Chandlerville, by Daniel Atterberry, Fiddler Bill Watkins, and Fiddler Jones here and there over Menard County. Over at the Berry or the Clary store there is storytelling, there is loud laughter. At the Rutledge Tavern the late guest may be telling of the antics of the Spoon River, or of a recent killing at Bernadotte. The water whispers as it goes over the New Salem dam, for at night the wheels of the mill are still. Tomorrow there may be work with the bull-tongue plow, with cutting wheat with the sickle, or with the cradle scythe; or with breaking ground, driving six or seven oxen hitched to the plow to tear and turn the tough sod of the prairie. Or there may be hunting.

For deer are in the Sangamon River bottoms, and also raccoons and opossums. Occasionally a bear is encountered, and there are foxes, panthers and wild cats, rabbits and wild turkeys and squirrels. Wolves are numerous. They are very destructive to sheep, pigs, calves and poultry, and even to young colts. Sometimes when driven by hunger they approach the houses on New Salem Hill and snatch their prey from under the very eyes of the villager. So a wolf hunt may be organized. A number of men with rifles get on horses and sally forth into the prairie along the edge of the woods. If the hunt be successful the wolves come forth in packs and race across the open spaces, as the hunters shoot at them. These wolf hunts, which were common then, must have been as exciting as English fox hunting, often celebrated in verse. A wolf hunt is a fresh theme and is American.

Fifty years ago people marveled at the changes that had come to pass in the preceding fifty years, and wondered what the next fifty years would have to show. They should be here to see. They could not believe their eyes. Somehow wild animal life has greatly diminished in Illinois, much more so than it has in upper New York and in Connecticut, where deer and pheasant are plentiful enough, and roam at will by the stone fences and over the fields. In Illinois the prairie chicken, one of the most delectable of wild birds, has almost vanished, while it was once in abundant numbers over the state, on Sandridge, about Clary's Grove and New Salem Hill. There are still a few deer along the Sangamon River, but the wolf and the fox have almost disappeared. They have been exterminated as thieves. There are but few wild turkeys left in Illinois, and not enough quail in the northern part to make quail hunting attractive. Once the fields about New Salem Hill and over Menard County were full of quail. New Salem had wild turkey on feast days, and as an article of diet it outranks the domestic turkey.

The Illinois River, the Sangamon River and the waters in the valleys about them had myriad ducks and geese in the days of New Salem. For that matter, they are rather plentiful yet in season. But then the canvasback, the mallard and teal, the wood duck, brant and geese came and went in great flocks. Many of them got into New Salem ovens cooked with lye hominy and dodgers. There was no hunger at New Salem and no doles. War and monopoly had not yet accomplished their deadly work. There is nothing more beautiful than a flock of wild geese flying under white clouds brightened by the moon, flying over the prairie to some home of reeds by the river.

For amusement at New Salem there was the debate at the near-by schoolhouse, or the temperance lecture, or the spelling match, or the revival, also called the "protracted meetings," both of the Hard-Shell and the Soft-Shell Baptists, and of the Methodists. Such ministers as Goodpasture and Berry, and Peter Cartwright, kept the spiritual state of the people duly stirred. Going in the stage from New Salem to Lewistown and the Spoon River country Cartwright tarried at the village on the Hill, and he was frequently there when campaigning for the legislature. By day the Clary Boys and the residents on the Hill played horseshoes, they ran foot races, they raced their horses, they wrestled and fought with fists, while the cooper's maul at Onstott's and the anvil at Miller's kept time to the drone of the mill by the river. Occasionally there was the political orator. Cartwright was one of these. And there were fiddler contests participated in by all the fiddlers of the surrounding country who contested with each other for prizes. There were days, too, for fishing in the river for crappies, bluegills, bass, pike, cats, blue and channel, carp and suckers, and other fish in which the river abounded. And there were hunting and fishing excursions to the Illinois River by Havana, about thirty miles north of the Hill, where the game was different in some particulars and the fish of greater variety and of better quality in those deeper waters.

Some of the people read books. They had the Bible, the *Columbian Orator,* and the English reader. It is inferable that a copy of Volney's *Ruins* was somewhere about in the possession of Jack Kelso, who had Burns and Shakespeare, according to all the reports. To lie under the oak trees and read was one of his chief delights. Evidently he had little to do with the churches. There was a Hard-Shell Baptist church near New Salem, but not in the village. It was about a mile away. Jack Kelso probably preferred to walk in the woods by the river than go to church. He must have felt that there were trivial proceedings going on there. For once Mentor Graham was expelled from the church for signing the temperance pledge, and on the same day a member of the church was turned out for getting drunk. Whereupon a tipsy wag arose in the church, and holding up a bottle of whisky, called out, "Brethering, you have turned out one member because he would not drink, and another because he got drunk, and now I want to ask a question. It is this: How much of the critter does one have to drink in order to remain in full fellowship in the church?" This was a poser that Jack Kelso might have put, but it wasn't he. Jack was too much taken with the woods, the river and the prairie, with bee hunting and squirrel hunting, with the reading of Shakespeare and Burns, to be interested in such speculations. He preferred to watch the hummingbird, to follow the flight of the crows, to listen to the larks on the prairie, or the cry of the kingfisher by the river, or the chatter of the wren. There were many thrushes about, filling the woods with melody. There was the fresh song of the blackbird in spring, and there were the sweet-voiced vireos, and the orioles. Kelso was not trying to get political office, he could make a living by catching fish and doing odd work about the village. Hence he did not go forth to fight Black Hawk. If ever there was a case where lies and fear, fear that descended to the depths of vilest cowardice, produced battle and bloodshed it was this Black Hawk scrimmage.

New Salem was the voting place of the precinct. At Richland, a village not far from New Salem, men enlisted for the Black Hawk War. The section of country around New Salem sent one hundred men. In Morgan County, where Jacksonville is located, a company was raised of which my grandfather Masters was a member. He was ashamed of his service in such a cause to the last day of his life. Black Hawk's miserable, half-starved Indians stood no chance against the militia of Illinois, against the federal troops in particular. These Illinois soldiers went forth richly supplied with food, and with whisky, and with almost matchless brutality they murdered truce messengers coming from Black Hawk with messages of peace, with words that strove to tell what Black Hawk meant and all that he meant: which was that he wanted corn, yes, corn from the land that had been taken away from him.

The New Salem company reported at Beardstown and marched from there to Oquawka, on the Mississippi River in Henderson County. Finally near Byron, in Ogle County, there was the bloodshed of Stillman's Run. The site of this battle is four miles from Byron. Here twelve soldiers were killed, and nine were buried on the site. The graves are marked with small flags. In the woods near by are the graves of other soldiers. Here is a fifty-foot monument of

HANNAH ARMSTRONG HAD BREEDING AND
WAS A WOMAN OF EXCELLENT CHARACTER

dark granite adorned with the figure of a citizen soldier.

In the New Salem contingent were W. G. Greene, David Pantier, of the Concord Church settlement. Jack Armstrong was made a sergeant. William Cullen Bryant, on the occasion of his visit to his brother John Howard Bryant, saw this rough squad. "They were a hard looking set of men," he wrote about them, "unkempt and unshaved, wearing shirts of dark calico, and sometimes calico capotes."

It is for us of this day to say whether we look with respect upon the stone at Stillman's Run with its inscriptions to these soldiers, or at the colossal figure of Black Hawk on the shores of the Rock River near Oregon. What could be quoted or invented for the conquerors of Black Hawk so appealing as the words of the Indian chief after he was vanquished? He said, "Rock River was a beautiful country. I loved my towns, my cornfields, and the home of my people. I fought for it. It is now yours, keep it, as we did."

It was the push of business that erased the village on the Hill. The Black Hawk War ended in driving all the Indians from Illinois. Then came the Mexican War, which broadened the American domain, and brought back majors and colonels from Cerro Gordo and Palo Alto, to stump about on one leg in Petersburg for the rest of their days. Ideas and feelings were abroad which made the past impossible to perpetuate. They ate at the shore of the times like water on a clay bank. The Conestoga wagon, which hauled by six horses supplied merchandise over the Allegheny Mountains was passing, and the Inn at Washington, Pennsylvania, where Henry Clay stopped on his way from the National Capital to his Kentucky home, was fading together with the decay of the old Proctor House in Lewistown. Petersburg was building a courthouse and stores about the square and houses of brick and frame on the hills. David Rutledge was practicing law in Petersburg.

New Salem as a poplar tree had thrived,
And aged too soon and died.
The three-faced camp, the hut of logs
With puncheon floor, and chimney contrived
Of mud, small sticks; the log schoolhouse,
The water mill by the river's side;
The mold board, shovel, and bull-tongue plows,
The hunter with his hunting dogs
Vanished away, and left a moon-haunted hill,
A soaring headland of trees,
Enchanted by the re-remembered stars,
To lapse to prairie dreams again
Amid autumnal wind and winter rain,
Rending the rumpled roof, the wasting sill.
Gone then the coopershop, the tannery,
The wheelwright, blacksmith, the village school,
The justice court were seen no more.
And overgrown was the trodden place
Where men played horeshoes, or came to race.
No more upon his smooth worn stool

The saddler sat. No more by night or afternoon
Men gathered at Berry's Store to talk and chaff
About the week's events, to talk and laugh
Of Clary's Grove, which in their idiom
Was the world to them,
Beyond which was no world at all.
They meet no more to dance the fiddle tune,
To wrestle on the grass,
To gossip by the moon,
To drink the friendly glass.
No more the husking bee, the apple festival.
No more to the Tavern table came
Rough-handed men, noisy with merriment,
In blue jeans, linsey-woolsey dressed.
Nor in the evening by the Tavern fire
Was there rejoicing that Jackson had restored
By his will and the people's word
The usury-bitten rights of the common man,
And given woodsmen, plowmen, their worthy hire,
And the soil its rulership by the plan
Of nature and the faith American.
No more by the hearth, which cast a bloom
Over the humble living room,
Was seen the family: the father bent
On making shoes, the mother at the loom,
The daughter at the wheel,
Which whirred its musical content,
While simmered on the crane the evening meal.

Before the Rutledge Tavern on the green
The dancers came as the rising moon
Soared from the river's coolness where the woods
Were deep in shadows strewn,
Like memories falling in revisited solitudes.

The fiddle here woke echoes sweet and keen,
Piercing the forest's hush, which else was still,
Save for the chanting of the whippoorwill,
And save for voices happy and murmurous
About the streets, by doorways; while the East
By soundless wings of light was fanned,
Which wafted an aureole more luminous
As the moon's less timid step released
The doors of the sky with aweless hand.
Those dancers gone, the eddying leaves,
With light from heaven twined
Danced to the fiddles of the wind.
And when the sun like tranquil thought,
Like flaming life to death resigned
Set on the prairie, and New Salem Hill
With silence and long level light was caught;
And when this life-deserted tavern hall
Stood silent and leaning, still
Soared up the moon, but only to enthrall
The ruin of a happiness with her glance
Upon hushed woods, and hearthstones cast
About the broken floor,
Upon the windowless window, and the door
With dumb and open mouth, speaking a past
Of laughter, the fiddle and the dance.

Goldsmith's Auburn was a place of deserted life. New Salem is the Hill once dedicated to America claiming a hemisphere to itself, with interests of its own, with security against alien quarrels and ideas in the unsophisticated minds of agrarian citizens, and in their manliness and independence. Their very ignorance was a block to the conspiracies against liberty coming from centers of Old World hate and greed. When the village of New Salem fell it was a sign and a symbol that the American idea was menaced. The village took the Hill for its place of burial, and no place could be more fittting, more beautiful. From the hill it is only a short distance across the prairie to Oakland Cemetery where Anne Rutledge found final burial, after lying in Old Concord Cemetery for over fifty years. We can go that way or down the Hill to the road that leads through Petersburg, thence up a hill and down a hill, and up another hill to Oakland under the oaks, where many from Sandridge and Clary's Grove and other parts of Menard County are at one with the grass and the flowers.

CHAPTER TEN

THE RISE of Springfield undoubtedly had its effect on New Salem. The distance between the two places, about twenty miles, in the days of Jack Kelso took the good part of a day, for the roads were bad. Now the distance can be covered in a few minutes. For Illinois has 13,000 miles of hard road. There are two ways to go, both good: One by the so-called Peoria and Springfield road, which does not pass through Petersburg, but to the east of it. This way one crosses the Sangamon River bridge, and goes up the hill past Wolf Fuelner's Old Brewery and Rose Hill, towards Greenview, then north on the hard road through Indian Point, where the buildings of the North Sangamon Academy stand in an oak grove to the right. The other way to Springfield is at the foot of the New Salem Hill, and leads along the river to the capital of Illinois, a city of over 70,000 people.

It is the largest city of the Sangamon River valley. In his last years William H. Herndon lived on a farm just a few miles north of Springfield, and there struggled with his biography of Lincoln, while practicing law in Petersburg. At one time he had been mayor of Springfield, and a lawyer of fairly profitable business there. Toward the eighteen-seventies he went into bankruptcy. His farm did not pay, and in the nature of things could not. For he was in the fifties by this time, and his intemperate habits had reduced his vitality. I fancy him somehow sitting at the window of his little farmhouse, looking over the Sangamon River country and thinking of the days when he was in partnership with Lincoln, days that had unfolded to the incredible pageant that he saw passing before him, as America changed. He and his little son died the same day about 1891, there in the farmhouse. He was buried in Oakland Cemetery, a beautiful spot near Springfield. In 1918 a stone was set up to his memory, amid ceremonies, a part of which was an oration pronounced by my father in honor of his old friend. I wish I could tell some of the Herndon stories, those in particular concerned with his abandoned humor and pranks at Petersburg in court there. They are not printable, despite their humor, they are as genuine as the frolics of Rabelais.

Instead of going to Springfield now, we can turn west after leaving New Salem and go to Beardstown on the Illinois River, not far from the place where the Sangamon River empties into the larger stream. Beardstown is noted for watermelons, fresh-water pearls and carp. In one year over a million pounds of carp were marketed there. The mussel shells of the Illinois River and the Sangamon River often contain pearls of great beauty and value, which along the years have been gathered by Italians living there and shipped to jewelers in Paris. If you go to Salem, Massachusetts, guides will point out to you the hill where the witches were hanged. At Beardstown they will show you the city hall where Duff Armstrong was tried for murder. It was built as the courthouse in 1845. Now it is a historic shrine, all because Duff Armstrong of Sandridge, and Mason County, was tried within its walls, and found not guilty of murdering a German named Metzger. The verdict was wet with tears for Aunt Hannah who would be deprived of her worthless boy if they hanged him or sent him to prison. Many murder cases were tried in the old courthouse at Lewistown as sensational, as perilous to handle as that of Duff Armstrong, but the setting was different and Lincoln was not in the case. It was just like all the trials of that sort in the Illinois of that time. They were distinguished by fervent appeals to the mercy of the jury, not to take the prisoner from the courtroom and choke him to death on the gallows. Why do so brutal a thing as that, and break the heart of a good old mother?

There was a man named Cassius Graccus Whitney who lived at Virginia, not far from Beardstown, a lawyer of almost magical skill. He came to Illinois from New York in the 1870's, when about twenty, and located in Perkin in Peoria County where he followed the trade of a cooper for a time, and then studied law and was admitted to the bar. Virginia was about to lose the county seat, and for the unheard-of fee of $13,000 he espoused the cause of Virginia. He won handily, as he did almost every case he handled. Along the years and in his later life, though he lived to be but forty or so, he was about the various county seats at court time, at Petersburg, Peoria, Virginia, and Lewistown where he lived last and where he died and was buried by the Masons, as he left not a cent. He went about picking up cases and at the last had no office and not a lawbook to his name. His phenomenal memory retained forever whatever he read. He knew where to find the law, when he needed to find it. He knew pages of Shakespeare, and at Lewistown and at other county seats when he was flush with a fee he stood at bars buying drinks for everyone and quoting Shakespeare and Milton. There were desperate clients here and there whose cases had been fumbled, or almost lost by local lawyers. When Cash Whitney arrived in a county seat the word went around, "Cash Whitney's in town." Then the distressed suitor would seek him out at one of the bars and unfold his tale of woe.

A doctor named Breeden was sued for slander at Lewistown, and his case was messed by the lawyers of the town. It was dangerous business. The case was serious and Breeden was rich. But Cash Whitney came to town, and Breeden went to him. Cash said, "I'll go to the clerk's office and look at the declaration." He did so and came back, saying, "I'll beat the case for a thousand dollars." Breeden squirmed, but had to submit. Cash went into court with a demurrer and in an argument that electrified the crowd persuaded the court to throw the case out. This is the kind of thing that he could do.

John Gumm was a very large landowner in Menard and Mason counties on the Sangamon and Illinois rivers. His son killed a man on the streets of Havana, and the father in despair sought out Cash Whitney, who had come to Havana to pick up what he could during the term of court. John Gumm met Cash on the street, and said, "My boy killed a man and I want you to defend him. What will you charge?" Cash said he would have to look at the indictment before he could say what his fee would be.

He went to the clerk's office and returned to Gumm, saying that he would acquit the boy for four thousand dollars. Gumm gasped for breath, explaining the amount of corn he would have to sell to get that much money. Cash admitted that this was so, but at the same time the boy was in jail and might be hanged. Gumm got the money at the bank, and Cash went into court and freed the son. Then he journeyed up to Peoria, always a sportive place, where he lost the whole fee at poker in a few hours. Broke, he returned to Havana, and soon met John Gumm, to whom he said, "John, I wish you'd pay me that five hundred dollars you owe me." Gumm was stupefied. "What five hundred dollars?" "That five hundred dollars you owe me for defending your boy." Whereupon Gumm became very angry. He said, "I paid you four thousand dollars, all you asked and an awful amount of money, and you won't get another cent from me." "Then I'll sue you," said Cash very blandly. And he did. Gumm employed the best lawyers he could get in Havana to defend the claim. Cash went on the witness stand and testified that the debt was due him for defending Gumm's boy. Then Gumm's lawyer swelled out pompously and asked Cash if Gumm had not paid him $4,000 for defending the boy. Cash coolly admitted that it was so. "Well, then," the lawyer proceeded confidently, "what is this five hundred dollars for?" "For framing the defense" answered Cash calmly. There had been rumors that the jury had been bribed. But now the judge smiled and then laughed. He couldn't help it. Cash got a verdict for $500, amid loud laughter in the courtroom.

Cash never lacked for business. At the last he lived in a small house in Lewistown with a woman of bad repute. His really beautiful wife, native to New York, left him as he sank more and more into dissolute ways. His health failed him, and he went about the square of Lewistown helped by a cane, still retaining his black curly hair, still looking with piercing eyes on the scene that he had helped to make more idiotic, more meaningless, still reciting Shakespeare in the saloons, still in possession of a kind of philosophy that could vent itself in sharp witticisms and humorous stories. When he lived at Pekin he was district attorney. He was then just over twenty-one years of age. That is the only office he ever held. He was as much without ambition as Bill McNamar.

Decatur is a city on the Sangamon River of about 60,000 people. It lies in a bend of the river. It is a prairie town resting on a long swell of grassland. It was founded in 1829. Thomas Lincoln settled twelve miles from the site of the town when he came from Indiana, and it was his first home in Illinois. The James Millikin University is located here, and there are factories and railroad shops. At the edge of the city is an artficial lake with twelve miles of shore line, and impounds eight billion gallons of water. It was made by damming the Sangamon at the cost of one million dollars. It furnishes to Decatur and the surrounding country facilities for sailboating, swimming and fishing, similar to those of Lake Springfield.

All this is very far from the pioneer days, and even very far from the trade dollar days, the jigsaw architecture of the Hayes period, the mounting capitalism of the Cleveland times. What happened to the Sangamon River country was not inevitable. It was only one of the things that could have happened, and being that, it was not fate. Men are always free to take several different roads, and when they talk about destiny they are often concealing what they want to do, so that others will not see that they want to do it. It is being forced upon them. There was no destiny about America's Philippine Adventure, no destiny about business centralization. But as Peoria, Springfield and Chicago began to crowd New Salem and the Sangamon country there was perhaps a destiny about their transformation.

The spirit of a people is perhaps the most precious thing of all human values. Something about the sky, the hills and prairies, the oak trees at New Salem and along the Sangamon River made the spirit of the people. Something about the paved roads along the river and the beauty of Lake Springfield make the spirit of the people today. And no one will say that it was more delightful to swim in the muddy Sangamon in the days of Dennis Hanks than to take a dip in a bathing suit in the good water of Lake Decatur or Lake Springfield. To have a meal from the hot coals of a New Salem hearth would be a novelty. But there at the Wagon Wheel Inn at the foot of the New Salem Hill it is possible to have steak or chops with salad and with coffee that has some strength of the berry, not coffee such as the country people knew long ago. Didn't people have enough of plugging along in wagons in mud up to the flanks of the horses? Could the pioneers but have seen a Ford or a Chevrolet skimming along Bowman's Lane in Sandridge, that lane that once was so heavy with mud in the winter season that only a horse bestridden by a volunteering neighbor could get to Petersburg once a week for the mail! In a car one can pass the woods near John McNamar's acres, and get the sweet air that issues from them, and with that air have visions of the past and of the future. Nature is eternal.

Hunting was doubtless more fun when deer were plentiful in the bottoms, when the swift prairie chicken roared through the sky over the hunter's head, as he did the best he could with one shot, and could not follow them with the shots of a repeater. But I should rather see Jack Dempsey or Joe Louis in one of their contests than to have witnessed the brutal fight with bare knuckles between Henry Clark and Ben Wilcox just below the dam at New Salem. That fight was a draw, and there is talk of it today around Petersburg by descendants of John Clary.

Wilcox died in a year after the fight. The terrible punishment he received from the square-jawed, powerful Henry Clark finished him. The face of Henry Clark shown in the local histories reveals a bulldog tenacity that would have put up some resistance to the skill of Jack Armstrong. Clark is reported in a biographical sketch as a prosperous farmer, as a man interested in all matters "pertaining to the good of the community, particularly in church and school affairs." He was a Kentuckian who in the New Salem days was a man twenty-five years of age.

Something has departed from the haunts of Shambolee and Shickshack, from the woods of Indian Creek, Rock Creek and Baker's Prairie, where Peter Cartwright howled salvation. The prairie and the trees strive to say what it is. Why concern ourselves with it when farmers at home can listen on the radio to concerts in Chicago or New York, and to news from Europe? Even newspapers have to step aside for the radio. Why pay for a newspaper when the news can be had for practically nothing, and had fresh and in dramatic fashion?

Before going to Springfield, the town that took Lincoln from New Salem in 1837 and settled Herndon as a lawyer, it might be well to follow Salt Creek briefly from its conjunction with the Sangamon River to its source in the wide and beautiful country of McLean County, thus passing through Logan County and Dewitt County, and up through the prairie where Bloomington sits in the pastureland. In Logan County lived Richard Oglesby, one of the governors of Illinois; and here William Scully from Ireland squatted in 1853 and became the owner of 50,000 acres of the fertile land of this county. In 1889 Illinois passed a law against the alien ownership of land. Scully circumvented the law by becoming a citizen.

But I'd rather speak of Tim Beach, who for long years lived in Lincoln, dying four or five years ago near ninety years of age. He was a hearty, humorous, hospitable man and a lawyer of power, really stemming from the able lawyers who traveled the Eighth Circuit. And in fact he traveled the circuit. His practice took him into Menard County, Mason County, and into faraway Fulton County. Wherever he went he was hailed at "Tim" and beseiged for stories. How shall he be classed? By what token shall he be remembered? There are many men who just draw a near-fame, who just touch greatness, and failing in the game of life to reach the goal sink away like weeds, perhaps to nourish the soil of a state's culture; indeed, to do that very thing. Tim Beach was one of these men, and so was my father, who was a lawyer of unexcelled ability, and a victor in some of the hardest cases that were ever handled in Illinois. He defended some of the most hopeless murder prosecutions in the history of the state, and he won the acquittal of the men charged with burning the old courthouse at Lewistown, and thereby saved for the old town the county-seatship. It is too long a story to tell here, but in brief, the prosecution depended solely on the confessions that the accused had made that they had set the building afire. According to the law, proof had to be made first outside of the confessions that someone had set it afire. That proof was lacking. All he did was to object to the admission of the confessions until that *aliunde* proof was made. The prosecution couldn't make it.

Bloomington, with its domed courthouse, its small skyscrapers, its very good hotels, its crowded streets, brings forgetfulness of Salt Creek and the prairie. But in a brief time you can drive from this congestion west to the limits of the city. There a fence is encountered, so definite is the boundary of the city. On the other side of the fence corn is growing, or corn is in shock.

Bloomington was the home of Judge David Davis, who held court here and there in the 1850's when lawyers traveled the circuit. Afterward he was a justice of the Supreme Court of the United States, and early in his life he became very rich. Here also lived Adlai E. Stevenson, a vice-president. Elbert Hubbard was born in Bloomington, and Richard Hovey came from McLean County, moved east and died at thirty-six after writing the most beautiful interpretations of the Arthurian legends that any American has done. When Robinson was delving in these old tales for plots no one seemed to remember that Richard Hovey had anticipated and surpassed him thirty years before.

In the cemetery of Bloomington was buried Marie Von Elsner, "Litta," the singer, a girl of poor and humble family there, with a voice of miraculous sweetness, of which experts made great predictions. By aid of people of Bloomington she received some training abroad, and returned to America, and entered upon a career in concert work and the opera. In the midst of rising fame and prosperity she died, worn out by efforts to finance her family. Ah, who remembers Litta now? The people of Bloomington do, and if you are looking about the town they will take you to her grave, marked by a stone that struck me as rather inappropriate. But does it matter? She didn't quite reach the heights. She was cut off in youth, and in a way belongs with the unremembered dust of Tim Beach, and of others who traced themselves around the more distinct figures of Life's weave.

> What is the end of fame? 'Tis but to fill
> A certain portion of uncertain paper.

With Litta and Tim Beach belongs my father, Hardin Masters, a wonderful lawyer, who for years in Lewistown befriended every victim of unfortunate circumstances, and did it nearly always without compensation. The desperate causes that he championed cannot be told here. His courage and his skill gave him notability in all the counties that surrounded Fulton County. His storytelling, his vital humor, his generosity and good will made him beloved above all men of his place, and took his name far up into Logan County where Tim Beach was his lifelong friend. Like all men of his kind, he was grossly misunderstood and savagely attacked by one of the papers of Lewistown, which always thirsted for the fruit of the scaffold. At last he was tucked under the grass of Oakland Cemetery; and the list grows shorter every year of those who remembered him. I was in Lewistown some years ago and went to the house that he had owned, asking to look at the little room in which I used to write when I was sixteen and seventeen. The woman who owned the house had never heard of him; and uptown I was scarcely able to find anyone to whom his name was familiar. Contrast this with the years of the 1890's when his name was on every tongue in the county.

You can get into your car at the Wagon Wheel Inn, at New Salem, and almost before you can settle yourself in the seat you are in Springfield, the magical city of Lindsay's imagination, the city he loved and toiled for and tried to rescue from what he thought was its materialism, its indifference to beauty and progress. Why didn't New Salem become a city instead of Springfield? The prairie to the west furnished ample space for houses and public buildings. The immediate country about it is more beautiful than that of Springfield. The river is at its very edge, at Springfield the river is a few miles away. The *Talisman* and the *Utility* docked at New Salem as well as at Springfield. New Salem had coal and stone at hand, and fertile, productive fields. Michigan City in Indiana once wondered why it didn't become Chicago, and how it lost the prize of being a metropolis. New Salem never wondered about the rise of Springfield. At the beginning the people felt the rival magnetism of Petersburg more than they did that of Springfield. In truth they moved to Petersburg with happiness, for the clock had struck and there was a courthouse building in Petersburg. It was on the river too, and familiar faces were at once about the square. They were still at home, as they might not have been among the Kelly colony, of North Carolina, which came to the Sangamon River country in 1818 and wandered through a land abounding in deer and wild turkey. They erected a strong log house, and cleared and cultivated some land, and feasted on the fish from the Sangamon River and the game from the bottoms. They became a settlement around which other settlers gathered. By the time Sangamon County was created in 1821 the Kelly colony was large enough to provide accommodations for the new county officials. There was a movement to call the place Calhoun, after the celebrated senator from South Carolina; but Spring Creek was near, and the Kelly fields were on the tongues of the people, so the town was called Springfield. In a corner of John Kelly's field a stake was driven, and he was commissioned to build a log courthouse with logs twenty feet long, and to to do it for $42.50.

There was Sangamo Town seven miles northwest of the Springfield site. Sangamo had wanted to be the county seat. But it was outwitted. The state capital was then at Vandalia, and a legislative committee came to decide between Sangamo and Springfield as the county seat. There was at Springfield a man named Andrew Elliott. He was a hunter and a woodsman who knew the bogs, the swamps and forests of the neighborhood. He became the guide of the legislative committee, and he led the lawmakers around and around, by wandering ways through slushy lowlands, through dense hazel thickets, and patches of giant weeds. He led them on until they were all but exhausted. They were covered with mud, their clothing was stuck full of burrs and beggar's lice. They saw Sangamo, and went to Springfield, deciding on the way that Springfield was more accessible than Sangamo. That ended Sangamo, and it vanished. There is not a trace of it today. Andrew Elliott had won, and maybe had tricked the committee.

Then came the adventure of the *Talisman.* By then there was a newspaper in Springfield called the *Sangamo Journal* and it spoke excitedly of the arrival of the *Talisman.* "Springfield can no longer be considered an inland town," it said. "We congratulate our farmers, our mechanics, our merchants and professional men for the rich harvest in prospect, and we cordially invite emigrating citizens from other states whether they be rich or poor, if so they be industrious and honest to come hither and partake of the good things of Sangamo." The navigation of the river failed. But the fertile land around Springfield did not fail, and there was coal under the site, and co-operating circumstances that began to push the town into the dimensions of a city. The Erie Canal came along, bringing tides of settlers to the rich soil of the Sangamon country. As New Salem had to endure the rise of Petersburg, Vandalia on the Kaskaskia River had to see the claims of Springfield for the capitalship of the state honored, as Lincoln and other members of the legislature by a huge logrolling, and a shrewd trading of votes in the interest of railroads and canals, wrested the statehouse from Vandalia. And it was not so very far at that from the center of the state, though Springfield is nearer to Chicago than Vandalia, and in the course of time that proved important. The truth is that Kentucky, Tennessee, Virginia and the Carolinas lost out all around as time went on. It looks like fate, but what is fate but the plans and schemes of men? Coal and corn helped Springfield, for shaft mines were sunk in 1867, railroads entered the town. In 1865, when Peoria tried to become the state capital, Springfield raised $200,000 for a new and finer statehouse, and held to its honor as the seat of state government.

The present Sangamon County Court House was the capitol of the state, built in 1837 and not abandoned as such for forty years. It stands in the center of Springfield, where the business district grew up around it. Its architecture is solid and dignified, as much of the public architecture was one hundred years ago. It is built of heavy stone, with a dignified dome, and projecting porticoes supported by huge columns of limestone, of Doric shape. It is a much better building than the old capitol at Vandalia. A modern city of tall buildings has gathered around it so that it stands dwarfed today, though it is a story taller than when first erected.

At the turn of the century there was a movement on foot to raze this beautiful structure and build a new courthouse, more adequate to the times. But a feeling for historical associations defeated the plan. Instead, additional rooms for public use were provided by jacking up the building and inserting another story under it. But that really destroyed the harmony of the structure. One is shocked to see the difference between the new stone and the time-stained and time-scarred stone of the edifice in which the celebrated men of the past argued causes and made speeches for the republic. The so-called new capitol, finished sixty years ago, stands on a rise of ground west of the square. It is of Renaissance architecture, and cost four million dollars, first and last, after considerable grafting and corruption. Around it have come the centennial building, the supreme court building and the building which houses the Illinois Historical Library, where everything pertaining to Illinois, including New Salem, can be consulted.

Naturally, Springfield is saturated with memory of Lincoln. His old residence is a memorial museum. It was in the old statehouse that he made the "Appeal to the People" in which he said, "These are bad times and seem out of joint. All seems dead, dead, dead; but the age is not dead; it liveth as sure as our Maker liveth. Under all this seeming want of life and motion the world does move nevertheless. Be hopeful. And now let us adjourn and appeal to the people." No one came to hear Lincoln make this speech but the faithful Herndon, and John Paine, the janitor of the building. Yes, the times are always out of joint, they are always dead, the republic is always perishing or ended. But nature is eternal, as Shelley sang when looking at the ruins of Rome. Men can be piled in death as thick as cordwood at Gettysburg, Verdun or in Flanders, the game of life is always taken care of by nature, and after all Rome never fell.

Out in Oak Ridge Cemetery is the Lincoln tomb which cost $200,000, finished in 1874. When it was being constructed a Methodist church was dedicated in Menard County at which Peter Cartwright was officiating. At the close of the ceremonies when a collection was asked to finish the church he said, "The people of the country are excited over the erection of a monument to Abe Lincoln at Springfield, and are contributing liberally of their means for its completion. This is all very well; but, my friends, I am engaged in building a monument to the Lord Jesus Christ. This monument is the house in which we are assembled, and I want you to contribute enough to complete it."

Of all native-born men Vachel Lindsay is Springfield's most important figure. He is the most important figure native to Illinois. His father and his father's father were Kentuckians; his mother was from central Indiana, where the country was much like that around Springfield. The poet grew up among people who still remembered the buffalo grass of the prairies, and the wolves and rattlesnakes that infested them. Springfield, like New Salem, had many Kentuckians, and there was talk about of Daniel Boone, and the log cabin joys of his day. Memory of the revivals, of the camp meetings survived, and Peter Cartwright remained a telling character. The poet heard tales of primitive weddings, of festivals and bee hunts, of the fiddlers and dancers of Sangamon County, of New Salem and its characters, like Jack Kelso and Mentor Graham, and of course of Lincoln. Lindsay was born in a house in Springfield which his father acquired at the time of his marriage, having at that time moved from Cotton Hill in Sangamon County. In that house he lived the greater part of his life, and he died in it after fifty-two years of troubled existence, in which his imagination tortured, yet sustained him. It is a respectable frame house not far from the courthouse, and still stands.

Byron was called by Shelley "the pilgrim of eternity"; Lindsay may well be remembered as "the lame boy seeking the shrine." After a tumultuous career in Springfield he went to Chicago to study art. He wanted to draw, to paint. Poetry at that time was a subordinate interest with him. His mother did not encourage him either as an artist or as a poet. His father was puzzled by his activities in the field of agitation and reform, and did not know what to do with him. He was earning nothing and had to be supported. He dreamed of angels, of heaven, of ships of love, of Johnny Appleseed, of a new Springfield of more beautiful architecture, of a finer aesthetic. He issued at his own expense for printing what he called *War Bulletins,* in which he summoned the people to rouse to a new day. The citizenry were offended, they disliked as well his temperance tracts and speeches. He worked in a department store in Chicago, and studied art there. In New York he was in the Chase School of Art, and he taught art in the Y.M.C.A. He wrote poems and walked up and down Ninth and Tenth avenues, into drugstores, restaurants, laundries, offering his poems for a few cents. In 1906 he went to Florida with a friend, intending to walk back. He did walk back as far as Orange, Indiana, where his grandmother lived. There his father and mother picked him up and took him to England and continental Europe. All the while he had ideas of beggary as a means of life, like St. Francis. His poetical imagination grew more and more to be like that of Blake. Back in Springfield again he started the *War Bulletins;* but he dropped them and issued *Vision, A Quarterly Journal of Aesthetic Appreciation of Life.* He was now preaching the New Localism.

In May of 1912 he started to walk from Springfield to Los Angeles, and to make his way by trading poems for meals and lodging. He made up a portmanteau of poems and pictures, and copies of the *Village Magazine,* another publication that he had founded. He was saying, "the love of beauty has two sides: the love of beauty and the love of God." Thus equipped, he walked out of Springfield. The first day he made twelve miles, at the end of another day he was on the Illinois River. On he went, crossing the Mississippi, traversing Missouri, entering Kansas. Oh, the long way, oh, the sunburnt men, oh, the endless fields of wheat! He worked in some of them too, he sawed wood and made garden for a piece of bread, a cup of coffee. He slept in woodsheds, in livery stables, on kitchen floors when he could not do better. Some people listened to him as he chanted his poems and gave him meals for copies of them. Others smiled on him with suspicion or contempt. He heard the Rachel

Jane sing in the hedges, the autos rushed past him and gave him material for the "Santa Fe Trail," the thunderheads soared over him in the hot skies. On he went, trusting in a something that makes for beauty in the world, and guards it from harm. He came at last to Granada, Colorado. He was tired, he had not slept well along the way, the people were not interested in the Gospel of Beauty, in his poems. Walking had lost most of its adventure, it was too much like routine. Ahead of him were still one thousand miles, mostly desert. To cross them and reach California was merely a stunt, like walking on his hands for a wager. Oh, the long way, the hot sun, the endless miles!

He was tired, his resolution failed him. He telegraphed to his father for money so that he could take the train to Los Angeles, and his father sent him $40, and he rode into that city. It was in late September.

Finally he got back to Springfield, where he wrote "General William Booth Enters Heaven." That made him famous. It did not lift from his frail shoulders the task of drudging and lecturing for a living. He was yoked to that for nearly twenty years longer, when he became utterly exhausted, and took leave of life by his own hand. Oh, the long, long way, the rain, the clouds, the wheeling buzzards overhead!

There should be a mural at New Salem representing Lindsay walking toward the setting sun, there or in one of the new buildings in Springfield. His New Localism was intended to be a recapture of the

Village on The Hill. His last poem was entitled "Mentor Graham, School Teacher One Hundred Years Ago." It was published in the *Illinois State Journal* of Springfield on November 8, 1931. A month later his body was in Oak Ridge, not far from the grave of Herndon, not far from the tomb of Lincoln. Many people had laughed at him, and winking tapped the skull. But it was seen by those who had eyes that he had given everything of his strength to his city. Men of prominence like Logan Hay raised a fund for his widow.

In 1930, Lake Springfield was commenced and finished in 1935. It covers over four thousand acres of ground, and by dams impounds the waters of Sugar Creek, which I believe is a tributary of the Sangamon River. The lake is many miles long and a mile or so broad, set in the prairie not far from Springfield. On one side of it is a naturally wooded park. Over it is the Vachel Lindsay Memorial Bridge, which connects the park with the west shore. At the far end of the bridge is a pedestal upon which there is a bust of Lindsay by Adrien Voisin. At last Springfield honored her poet, who was the flowering of New Salem, of the American idea which New Salem lived through the Clarys, the Rutledges and Jack Kelso. Vachel Lindsay was the full blossom of all this. He turned the fiddle into the lyre, the country reel to aesthetic dancing, the songs of the Cumberland Presbyterians to lyrics about Johnny Appleseed and the

American heroes. Jack Kelso read Burns's songs. Lindsay wrote songs for the Illinois country, as Burns had written songs for his village in Scotland. His dreams came out of the Sangamon River country. His classical dictionary was the tales of the prairies and their people. He wanted to make an Athens of Springfield, saying that Athens was not of great proportions and population, but was a thing of beauty. So it could be with Springfield. He protested all his life long against the merchant philosophy that has turned America into the hateful paths of empire, and subdued it to the feet of swine. New Salem is the village deserted by the pristine vision of the republic. Lindsay knew this and sang a requiem to the past.

Who knows whether his work will do anything for the restoration of that America which was symbolized by New Salem?

For at the time that Springfield was building Peoria was expanding. In 1835 when it was incorporated it had a population of more than 500 people; a decade later it had grown to 2,000, and by 1845 it had a city charter. The surrounding country gave it rye and corn, which were sacrificed to Bacchus, not to Ceres or Proserpine. It grew till it became the largest city of the Illinois River Basin. It distanced Bloomington, Decatur, also in the basin. Galesburg, which is to the west, is the place where they broke the prairie in more senses than one and where section hands, Swedes and Calvinism prevailed. There you look at the prairie from railroad shops. Galesburg is as different from Springfield, from the culture of New Salem, as Oslo is different from the Romantic Rhine, or Brittany, or Wessex. It is altogether different from Peoria; for in truth Illinois has sections of life, of human psychology, even as it has river lands, uplands, prairies and woodlands.

A flavor of romance is over the story of Peoria, even if it can't be detected amid the smell of its distilleries, the noise of its small metropolitan activity. It is now a city of more than 100,000 and the second city in size in Illinois. The French explorers were here in the seventeenth century, such as Marquette and Joliet, exploring the Illinois River and Lake Peoria, which is fed by the river. In the days of the Indians it was called Pimiteoui, which means fat lake. Fort Pimiteoui was built here in 1691, and a settlement grew up around the fort, which is the basis for the claim of Peoria that it is the oldest city in Illinois, older than Cahokia. Here was a friendly tribe of Indians, and as the place had river transportation it thrived as a trading post. The settlement was virtually abandoned during the Revolutionary War; after that the French returned and took up trading, which was continued into the period of American supremacy.

George Rogers Clark visited Peoria Lake during the Revolution and destroyed the Indian village. In 1781 a company of Spaniards, French and Indians came up the Illinois River to the lake and from there crossed to St. Joseph, Michigan, a territory of a still different quality. Peoria was called by the French Au Pé, Le Pé, Oypa and Au Pay, and finally referred to as Piorias. In 1813 Americans erected Fort Clark on the site of Au Pé, a forerunner of Clark's Pure Rye, whether actually connected with that product as a matter of naming or not. Steamboats found it a considerable cluster of cabins in 1828. By the forties it embarked in the manufacture of plows and threshing machines. By 1860 it had seven distilleries. In 1880 it was in the grip of the Whisky Trust. Prohibition quieted the stills, but the workers were absorbed for the time by other industries. When prohibition was repealed there was nothing necessary but to light the fires and let the steam from the mashes turn to whisky in the coils. Peoria went forward more prosperously than ever.

The flavor of old times is over Peoria. Starved Rock is not so very far away, the Illinois River is picturesque, the Spoon River and the old country about Lewistown can be reached in less than an hour by automobile. But of all the towns of the Illinois River Basin, Springfield is the most interesting, granting to Peoria all that it can claim from the fact that Marquette and the other French explorers roamed about it often and thoroughly, and did not see the site of Springfield, or look upon the waters of the Sangamon River. Peoria has the Illinois River and the bluffs, it is in a more scenic country than Springfield. For the Sangamon near Springfield is muddy and ugly, overshadowed by cottonwood trees, and lined with huge weeds. The prairie about Springfield has little or no diversity. Yet it is men, it is the human spirit that makes a city. And I can think of few, if any, men of distinction who were identified with Peoria, while Springfield is rich in historic characters. Robert G. Ingersoll is perhaps Peoria's most notable figure. But he was not born there. He lived there for a time, then removed to Washington and New York. While he was there he furnished vast amusement by his railleries, stories and what were considered his blasphemies. Often he was in Lewistown, trying cases in the old courthouse in the neighborhood of Spoon River.

The country both on the Sangamon and on the Spoon River is all different from New England in its beauty. For that matter passing from the desert near Mason City to the heights about Oregon on the Rock River, you might well imagine that you had gone to another state. Oregon has an altitude of over seven hundred feet, which is something for Illinois, and it is in a territory of hills and rolling uplands where there are many kinds of trees, for Illinois has 133 different varieties of trees, ranging from white pine to locust, maples, oaks, hickories, cherries and walnuts. The Rock River is truly beautiful, with its bluff called Eagle's Nest, so named by Margaret Fuller who said of the site that "Florence and Rome are suburbs compared to this Capital of Nature's art." It was fitting that Lorado Taft's 48-foot statue to Black Hawk was erected here. There it stands looking down upon the river and over the country with memorial eyes, such as the Indian chief had in life when mourning for his lost home. Near by is the Eagle's Nest Art Colony, frequented by Ralph Clarkson, the painter, and by Henry B. Fuller and Harriet Monroe and Hamlin Garland, to mention the better known people who made it a place of pilgrimage. The Sangamon River never had such spirits; it never had such a village as Grand Detour, so named by the French traders, where there is a quaint inn and many houses more than a century old shaded by ancient elms. New Salem was different.

How different all this from Mason City near 179,000 acres of desert, where not a weed grows and which the crows avoid for fear of perishing of thirst and hunger. How different from Tallula, which means "dropping water" in the Indian language. There is great variety of villages and spots in Illinois ranging from the Black Hawk country to New Salem, to old Vandalia, to Cahokia, to Nauvoo, where the Mormons settled and built a temple, then vanished to Utah when their leader Joseph Smith was brutally killed by a mob at Carthage.

In 1837 Springfield was a prairie village, such as Pleasant Plains is today, but having won the prize of being the capital of Illinois it began to grow, it soon had residences like the very respectable house of Lincoln, which became a two-story structure one time when Lincoln was away from home and his wife took it in hand to reconstruct the house into fitting proportions. It had the dignified brick house of Benjamin S. Edwards, which is now the Art Association Building, with a gallery of pictures on one floor and studios and classrooms on another. With the building of the capitol came the erection of a mansion for the governor, and two-story structures around the square where business was conducted, and in the upper rooms of which the lawyers and doctors carried on their professions. Lincoln and Herndon had their law office over the store of Joshua Speed. The site is now occupied by the large Myers Building. And hotels came along, such as the Globe Tavern, where Lincoln first lived after his marriage, paying $4 a week for the board of himself and bride. And of course churches were built. All this while New Salem, like a tired man sleeping by the roadside, surrendered itself to dust and cobwebs.

There were the roaring days of the War Between the States, and the middle years of the 1880's and the 1890's, when Springfield was a city of 40,000 or so, where the legislature met, bringing all sorts of characters from Chicago at the north, and from the Spoon River country from the northwest. They went to the statehouse and voted for foolish laws, and they got perquisites from the railroads, as well as passes for themselves and friends. They were herded by lobbyists, who used their resemblance to Lincoln to deceive the people, on the one hand, and to walk unsuspected of their machinations in the lobbies of the hotels, on the other. Poker and gambling throve everywhere, and there were places of vice in plenty along the right of way of the railroads.

When the legislature met there was great excitement in Springfield. The St. Nicholas Hotel and the Old Leland were the centers of interest, for in one the Democratic members stopped and in the other the Republican. What a throng in either lobby! Cigar smoke, tobacco chewing, a Babel of talk, frequent repairing to the bar for Old Crow, for old-fashioned cocktails. The dining room served at noon a course dinner which started with soup and pickles and ranged through roast beef, roast game, ham and what not, to ice cream and pie, with rutabagas, potatoes, turnips and mustard greens between. Such days! Such characters, like Phocion Howard, of Danville, who raised frogs for the market and wrote funny pieces for the newspapers; like S. P. Cummings, of Vermont, near the Spoon River, who could be seen in the lobby of the St. Nicholas stroking his goatee as he buttonholed a member of the legislature, and "discussed" with him the wisdom of certain pending legislation. And there was Lute C. Breeden, a gay-hearted, handsome, generous member from Lewis-

THE GENIUS THAT DEFINES MEN AND SPOTS OF EARTH

AS LAID ITS HAND UPON THE SANGAMON RIVER

town; and an astute member named Arthur Leeper, from Virginia near the Sangamon, moving about, taking drinks, talking and waiting for dinner. It used to be supposed that men died from drinking whisky; now it is known that they die from the hurt which drives them to whisky for a nepenthe. These men were enduring defeated life purposes; they were bored. This is not the Tabard Inn of Chaucer, nor the Rutledge Tavern of New Salem where the fiddlers played and men came to the table of roast duck in linsey-woolsey with appetites sharpened by labor with the ax in the fresh air, and with grimed hands. In the seventies the claims of the Illinois Central to land along Lake Michigan, in Chicago, had to be adjusted; they had to be adjusted later at the turn of the century. The street railroads of Chicago needed legislative help. Meantime John Gumm was raising corn on the Sangamon River bottoms; George Kirby was planting and cursing the rain, and Squire Masters looked apprehensively at the hot sky and wondered about his corn. One night a cyclone almost destroyed his house and barn, and he had to get money to restore them. All this while the members of the legislature worked their jaws and played poker and gorged on the noon-day meal at the St. Nicholas and the Leland.

Governor Altgeld made something of a change in all this idle manuvering. His stern and serious administration, his economic messages had their effect.

He vetoed many crooked bills and fought monopoly at every turn. What had become of the Andrew Jackson spirit of New Salem that he had to do this? In time the Leland was torn down and a better hotel built. The Abraham Lincoln Hotel made its metropolitan appearance, and the St. Nicholas became lost amid improvements and additions. Streamlined legislators took the place of the old horse-and-buggy crowd, of the crowd that belonged to the locomotive with a huge smokestack, and the small wooden cars.

Since 1893 the State Fair has been held at Springfield, and it is one of the largest in the whole country. The grounds contain 376 acres at the northern limits of the city. The event is attended by farmers from all parts of the state to see the display of stock and crops, to watch the races, and to hear the political haranguers who make the event an occasion to advance their pursuit of office.

Springfield still is growing faster than Bloomington and Decatur. It has good libraries, state and municipal, its art museums, its theaters and hotels, give it the advantages of a city. It has beautiful parks, and residential districts of handsome houses where the streets are tree lined. It has business too, as it makes flour, manufactures boots and shoes, watches and electrical machinery, and smelts zinc. For there are many zinc mines in Illinois, and latterly oil has been found in lower Illinois. That the Sangamon River is not navigable makes no difference with the prosperity of Springfield, or with its happiness. For sailboats and launches can be run on Lake Springfield, as years ago Henry Zoll, who owned the mill at Bernadotte, ran a small steamer up the Spoon River from the dam for the delight of his friends gazing at the wooded hills and the uplands of farms along the way.

Springfield is so congested with cars that you cannot tell but what you are in a crowded part of Chicago or New York. Parking facilities are pressed to take care of the numerous cars that have to pause here and there. The streets are crowded with people, and to cross them is hazardous, as it is in all the cities. When Herndon was mayor of Springfield there was plenty of room for buggies and wagons. Pedestrians could cross the streets anywhere, without looking to the right or to the left, even as they could in New Salem. Now they can scarcely do this in Petersburg. The day when people are piled up, as Thomas Jefferson said in his prediction about America when the cities would be populous and crowded, has come to pass, swiftly too, seeing that gasoline and the motorcar have complicated the transformation.

In the capitol, at the base of the inner dome, is a frieze which depicts scenes of the history of the state, together with statues near the peak of the rotunda of prominent figures of the state. The work was done by an artist named F. Nicolai, who died before he completed it. Also the panels which supplemented the panels of the frieze had not been placed in proper sequence. The artist left no key to his work, so that it cannot be finished as he conceived it. But that may be as well, for history is still unfolding, and juster views of men of the past are coming to pass. In time to come there may be on the grounds or in the rotunda a fitting statue to Stephen A. Douglas, a man of genius in the field of statesmanship in his day who very greatly overtopped all the senators sent to Washington. He was a mind of forthright honesty and dauntless courage. Memory may well arise to say that he was a builder of railroads, a true servant of civilization in the West, an orator of surpassing power, the founder of Chicago University, and a man who strove for the peace of his country. One of those storms of passion that take human beings swept him down, five years before an assassin took Lincoln from a world that is always troubled. Lindsay may get a statue in bronze somewhere on the lawn of the capitol grounds, and John P. Altgeld who was so brutally assailed and so ignorantly misunderstood East and West, and by some people of standing at that, when all the time he stood resolutely for what is now known to be the truth. This is the old story of men and life, and the fact that such misjudgments and rejections take place in one century teaches the world nothing about preventing them in the next. We can rise above such regrets by going to one of the circular windows of the dome and looking north over the city to the Sangamon River, and trace it till the eye seems to rest near the village on New Salem Hill.

On February 11, 1861, when Lincoln was leaving Springfield to take up his duties as president at Washington, he stood on the platform of the train and addressed the crowd which had gathered to bid him farewell. A few matters of fact must be assembled here to get the significance of his tribute on this occasion to the people of Sangamon County. In 1830 Sangamon County had a population of over 12,000 people. At that time New Salem was in Sangamon County, and did not become a village of Menard County until 1839. In whatever county it was in 1830, and before, its people and the people of Springfield were one people. They were from Kentucky and Tennessee and Virginia. In New Salem they had elected Lincoln captain of the volunteer company that set forth for the Black Hawk War. In 1832 Lincoln ran for the legislature, and at the New Salem polls he received 205 votes out of a possible 208. The rest of Sangamon County rejected him, and he was defeated. New Salem made him its postmaster in 1833. Then in 1834, while still a resident of New Salem, he ran for the legislature again and was elected. Though New Salem and Sangamon County were Democratic, Lincoln's popularity with the people, with the farmers and hunters of Clary's Grove, with the storekeepers, millers and fishermen of New Salem carried him to success. So it was that in sadly parting from Springfield he said, "To this place and the kindness of these people I owe everything." That was Lincoln's characterization of the Clarys, the Rutledges, the Greenes, and of Justice Green, of Jack Kelso, Henry Onstott, and of Jack Armstrong and his wife Hannah, of the Watkins families, and of Jimmy Short, of New Salem and Sandridge. With that generous friendliness that distinguished them up and down the Sangamon River they had helped Lincoln, and he knew it and fittingly acknowledged his indebtedness to them.

They believed in him as a man of their own blood, their own spiritual accent. He saw in them the quality of kindred souls. It was thus that New Salem on the Sangamon River was a flowering of American culture, such as never anywhere occurred in the land before or since.

The Sangamon River! What is the Sangamon River but the people who lived and toiled along its winding course? What would Ayr be in the way of a place, a something to be remembered, were it not for Robert Burns? It has numerous manufactures, it imports timber from Canada and Norway, something mentioned by way of distinction in books. Yes, but here Burns wandered, and his songs give it a place in time, and nothing else does. The flavor of his genius is memorably over the land.

> Petrarch's Vaucluse makes proud the Sorgue,
> Your Morgue has made the Seine renowned.

HE LEFT NO MEMORIAL TO HIMSELF IN NEW SALEM, EXCEPT IN THE ATTITUDE OF THE PEOPLE TOWARD HIM

The Sangamon River! Not navigable, not noted for its commercial activity, not distinguished for majestic scenery, nor for a battle, nor for a single historic event, distinguished for nothing but for good and useful lives lived along its shores, and for the beauty of its prairies that sleep and bloom and wave their grasses to the passing winds. It flows along where fiddlers lived, where little villages slept, mesmerized by time, where men came and went unnoted and unsung, many of whom fought the wars, and returned home crippled, or were sent back to be buried in Old Concord Cemetery, and in the old cemetery of Petersburg, above the river.

There were men at New Salem like T. W. McNeely and William G. Greene who became well known. But New Salem Hill would still be part of the prairie, the Rutledge Tavern would never have been restored, the house of Jack Kelso would have remained a vanishing memory, had it not been for an event which at the time was trifling, and for long years remained a neighborhood tale. That event was the fact that one day a "long, bony sad man floated down the Sangamon River in a frail canoe. Like a piece of driftwood he lodged at last" on the dam "Without a history, strange, penniless and alone." These are the words of Herndon. But suppose there had been no dam, no village of kind and hearty people up the hill, no Rutledge Inn, no fiddlers, no Bowling Green, no Jack Kelso, no Hannah Armstrong with whom to mingle what was kindred in him with their lives and with the dreams of Indian Creek and Sandridge? Suppose the people of the village had turned the wanderer away instead of taking him into their hospitality? Suppose they had not sustained him economically, and sent him to the Illinois legislature, and given him leisure to read Blackstone under the oak trees; in such case what would the memory of New Salem have been? He built no house, he left no memorial to himself in New Salem, except in the attitude of the people toward him, and their benefactions in his behalf, and the belief that grew up that he was like them. He was identified with the village about six years, while for twenty years he was about the streets of Petersburg in court time, and in the old courthouse trying cases for Mrs. Bowling Green, Squire Davis Masters and others. Who cares about that compared to his life in a happy village of Kentucky and Tennessee blood where Jack Kelso fished and hunted for a living, where Harvey Ross brought the mail on horseback from Springfield on his way to Lewistown and the Spoon River country, where the Clary's Grove boys rode into town and assembled at the grocery store for drinks and talk? Without these people, without what they were to Lincoln, the New Salem Hill would be covered with grass and prairie flowers, its log house sites would be sunk in undistinguishable growths of hazel and weeds, even as it was for seventy years after the disappearance of Jack Kelso, and until the people of Petersburg gathered up the remains of the past. Olympian Zeus was the friend of the stranger, the wanderer; and Fate has remembered the village that by a kind of genius received Lincoln and sustained him.

Contrast the names of the precincts of Menard County with the names of the townships of Fulton County, which is the Spoon River domain. It is evident at once that the people of the latter were under different traditional influences. Take Bernadotte: just why the people named the village and the township after one of Napoleon's favorites, I do not know. Why another township was named Astoria, as the city of Oregon named itself after John Jacob Astor, is also a question. Vermont Township evidently goes back to the state of that name, and Waterford to Waterford County in Ireland, and Joshua to some Biblical connotation, and Putnam perhaps to Israel of Revolutionary fame.

There was a time when China furnished names to towns over America. In Illinois there are Pekin on the Illinois River, and Canton in Fulton County, as well as Cuba near the Spoon River, which went to the Caribbean for a name. The only township names in Fulton County that sound like the names of Menard County are Pleasant, Fairview, Deerfield, Buckheart. In the latter grew up a mining town called Dunfermline. Then there are the township and river town called Liverpool. At one time it was of considerable importance, for the steamboats docked there. It was a depot at which to transfer goods to Canton and Lewistown and to Fulton County in general. Now it is a fishing port and the center of fine hunting grounds. Some of the landowners in Liverpool were Pollitt, Gustine, McCracken, Wilcoxen, Shufflebam. The Illinois River made the Spoon River country more accessible to Peoria than Menard County was, and that town, which became a city, more or less dominated the Spoon River country. Besides all this, the people of Fulton County, of the Illinois and Spoon rivers, were of different quality from those of Menard County. The distance between the two counties is short, but for that matter there might be camps of people a mile apart in the same woods, one speaking one language and one another, one living and feeling one way and one quite a different way.

There were a good many people in Fulton County from the South, but not enough to control the spiritual quality of the population. And there was no Cumberland Presbyterian Church. Liverpool never had a chance to become a New Salem, a village among oak trees on a river hill, and a memory forever. At New Salem men wrestled and fought with fists. At Bernadotte and Waterford they used knives and brassknucks and pistols. Nearly every term of court at Lewistown had one murder trial. There were not many murders in Menard County. Yet Menard

County hanged an insane man who killed his wife, while Fulton County had no hangings, at least none for fifty years or more. Menard County, of the Sangamon, seems never to have flourished in grudges, which broke forth after years of their germination in a killing. Fulton County had fiddlers and rowdy dances where there was insane drinking and stabbing. A man named Oscar Cox cut a fiddler to shreds at a dance in Waterford. He was arrested by a cousin, who was the constable of Waterford. Years after this when the two were driving home from Havana the constable got out of the wagon to open a gate. Cox leaped out and took after the constable with a knife to avenge his old grudge, all without any warning. The constable picked up a piece of a rail and struck Cox on the bridge of the nose. Cox fell dead then and there.

One of the terrible roughs of Bernadotte came one day to Marietta, in Harris Township, to kill a doctor there. The doctor's son stepped to the sidewalk when he saw the wild man approaching and blew him to pieces with a shotgun. One time I attended a country dance at Bernadotte. In the middle of the gaieties bricks crashed against the door and the windows. Soon a crowd of rough men crazed with whisky entered the room and broke up the dance. The Clary boys were wild enough, but I never knew them to act in this way.

Fulton County, the Spoon River country, is prairie land north of Lewistown, and around Canton and Fairview—but there are hills and broken valleys, toward the Spoon River, and toward the Illinois River east of Lewistown. In 1880 Lewistown built a narrow-gauge railroad from Galesburg to Havana. This was done to keep Canton from taking the county seat away from the old historic town. This ludicrous little road twisted and wound its way through the hills of Big Creek, turning every way in order to avoid the expense of cuts. On the lowlands below Lewistown it dodged here and there on a track that seemed like two streaks of rust. Its small engine with a whistle like a huge mogul made the valleys and the bottoms resound; for it was careful to warn straying cattle, and even heedless turkeys, and would often stop in order not to strike them. It ran near little towns like Ellisville, London Mills and Cuba; the first two were on the Spoon River, the last was near it.

This was a yeasty country. It had no Concord Church. Its prairies never seemed sunlit with that kind of light that seems supernal, the meadow larks sang as if they pined for the fields around New Salem. It was mental, not spiritual, if I may apply the word "mental" to circumstances and human beings such as are now imperfectly described. The genius that defines men and spots of earth, and chooses them for memory has laid its hand upon the Sangamon River and upon the village of New Salem. Their voice is the song of the meadow lark.

Meadow larks by Jimmie Miles',
All along the Bowman Lane,
In the sunlit hours complain,
Haunters of the airy aisles.

Horizon strips of forestry
Rim the fields of wheat and corn,
There the meadow larks forlorn
Hide in light their mourning cry.

Into groves of walnut cool
Pass we to the Sandridge land,
Over Concord parched to sand
Pass we where the sky is full,

Where the clouds of August soar,
And the schoolhouse in a trance
Looks upon the green expanse,
All along the Lattimore.

There where clover scents are blown
Still is wafted their refrain,
As it was in Bowman's Lane,
Spirits singing as if alone.

Orchards roaring in the breeze
Carry far and carry near
By the fields of Oscar Spear
Chorals of the earth's unease.

On the hill the well-loved house,
And the barn before us rise.
Here amid the westering skies
Song translates the apple boughs.

Generations past compute
Of these meadow larks have flown;
But their memory lives on,
Not in memory being mute.

Home forsakers and exiles
In imagination hear
How their children's song is clear,
Haunting still the airy aisles.

From the meadows by Salem Hill
Still the larks sing, still they soar,
With a cry which means no more
Do they wake the whippoorwill.

Do they chaunt the elegy
Of a people gone away,
Of a freedom and a day
Blest by woodland liberty.

And by Oakland, near and far
Do they voice eternal peace,
Till the sounds of labor cease,
Ended by the evening star.

Well, I must go on with this a little and amend somewhat, to say that Bill McNamar is the genius of the Sangamon River and the surrounding country. I am not speaking disrespectfully of the country, for I could call him the genius of life itself. I am hinting at phantom secrets, esoteric things, things that flash by and can't be described. I believe that Bill never learned to read and write, so it was that he didn't have to keep up with the flow of books, which do flow and pass for good and accomplish nothing. Bill went to the Shipley District School for a while, where the boys teased him, and where he sat like a frog in a trance looking with one eye at Jane Rodeman. He went swinging along over hill and dale, carrying his dinner bucket, and saying "howdy" to people that he passed. He never had problems, such as: is there life after death, has the universe a purpose, does that purpose notice man, is evil negative and good positive, is matter eternal, is God a person, or a blind creative force? Seeing that those of us who can read know nothing of these things, was it a misfortune for Bill that he was farther along in idiocy and didn't even know that there were such questions? Shakespeare had an understanding of the idiotic mind above everyone, and he loved idiots. He would have loved Bill as a blessed neutrality, and inspired nothing, whose word was always "maybe." So was Shakespeare's word always "maybe." Yes, he was "fifty, sixty, seventy, maybe." I often think of him there in the darkness of Bowman Lane singing "I Will Arise and Go to Jesus," so that his voice carried and wavered over the fields and into the woods. I believe if you went to Menard County and drove around the Sangamon, up into Sandridge where Dodson's slough is, where Buddy Traylor had a farm and then lost it by an idiotic turn of fortune, that there you might feel some strange presence. And it would be Bill Mc-

Namar, a something that is mixed with the sunlit west, the song of the lark and the stillness of fields.

Night came on. The windows grew black, I had to step to the casement to see the ailanthus tree in the court. Again time for bed, and I crawled in. No sooner, it seemed, did I touch the pillow than I heard a voice. I looked up and saw a figure crouched down near me. He was a ragged outline. His hat was drawn down over his face. He summoned me to get up, and when I did so he beckoned me to follow him. We went together out into the street, finally into the Holland Tunnel, then like shadows we moved swiftly through Plainfield, Somerville, town after town, huddled in darkness, on and on. Suddenly the Mason County desert, then the ruined shacks of Huron, then the Estill Hill, with Petersburg asleep at its foot. Then through the town, silent as space, then by the Charter Oak Mill, and out the New Salem road past the spot where the house of Bowling Green stood. By this time I realized where I was going, for in a trice we were walking up the hill to the village of New Salem. Still I didn't know who my companion was. In all this long jaunt of more than a thousand miles he had not once shown me his face. Now there were loud voices, singing, and the sound of hoofs of horses clattering away into the distance, as men called back good night. Not a word from my companion! As for me everything seemed natural enough. We came to the hill over Jack Kelso's Hollow, and there we sat down. What stillness about! Suddenly a wind tossed up the tops of the oak trees, and just then the moon broke from a cloud and flooded the face of my companion with light. I looked at him now. It was Bill McNamar, the Sandridge idiot. I looked and saw the Sangamon River twisting its way between the trees. I looked at my companion. His eyes were glowing like a fen-fire. He didn't speak. He tried to sing, but his voice choked. Then he got up and walked away, disappeared and left me there alone. Alone again! And there on the New Salem Hill, by the Sangamon.

INDEX